THE BEST OF
E. M. BOUNDS

THE BEST OF
E. M. BOUNDS

BAKER BOOK HOUSE
Grand Rapids, Michigan 49506

Copyright 1981 by Baker Book House Company

ISBN: 0-8010-0808-5

Compiled by Cornelius Zylstra

NOTE: At the time of his death E. M. Bounds requested that Homer
W. Hodge edit and publish a large collection of Bounds' manuscripts.
Eleven volumes of Bounds' writings were published under Hodge's
editorship, from which the selections were made for this book.

Cornelius Zylstra

PHOTOLITHOPRINTED BY CUSHING - MALLOY, INC.
ANN ARBOR, MICHIGAN, UNITED STATES OF AMERICA

Contents

THE BEST OF
E. M. BOUNDS

Excerpts from

The Necessity of Prayer

Prayer and the Word of God
Prayer and Faith

1
Prayer and the Word of God

How constantly, in the Scriptures, do we encounter
such words as 'field,' 'seed,' 'sower,' 'reaper,'
'seedtime,' 'harvest'! Employing such metaphors
interprets a fact of nature by a parable of grace.
The field is the world and the good seed is the
Word of God. Whether the Word be spoken or
written, it is the power of God unto salvation. In
our work of evangelism, the whole world is our
field, every creature the object of effort and every
book and tract, a seed of God.—David Fant, Jr.

God's Word is a record of prayer—of praying
men and their achievements, of the divine warrant of
prayer and of the encouragement given to those who
pray. No one can read the instances, commands, examples, multiform statements which concern themselves
with prayer without realizing that the cause of God, and
the success of His work in this world, is committed to
prayer; that praying men have been God's vicegerents on
earth; that prayerless men have never been used of Him.

11

A reverence for God's holy name is closely related to a high regard for His Word. This hallowing of God's name; the ability to do His will on earth, as it is done in heaven; the establishment and glory of God's kingdom, are as much involved in prayer, as when Jesus taught men the Universal Prayer. That "men ought always to pray and not to faint," is as fundamental to God's cause today as when Jesus Christ enshrined that great truth in the immortal settings of the Parable of the Importunate Widow.

As God's house is called "the house of prayer" because prayer is the most important of its holy offices, so by the same token the Bible may be called the Book of Prayer. Prayer is the great theme and content of its message to mankind.

God's Word is the basis, as it is the directory of the prayer of faith. "Let the word of Christ dwell in you richly in all wisdom;" says St. Paul, "teaching and admonishing one another in psalms and hymns and spiritual songs, singing with grace in your hearts to the Lord" (Col. 3:16).

As this Word of Christ dwelling in us richly is transmuted and assimilated, it issues in praying. Faith is constructed of the Word and the Spirit, and faith is the body and substance of prayer.

In many of its aspects, prayer is dependent upon the Word of God. Jesus says:

> If ye abide in me, and my words abide in you, ye shall ask what ye will, and it shall be done unto you (John 15:7).

The Word of God is the fulcrum upon which the lever of prayer is placed, and by which things are mightily moved. God has committed Himself, His purpose, and His promise to prayer. His Word becomes the basis, the inspiration of our praying, and there are circumstances under which, by importunate prayer, we may obtain an addition or an enlargement of His promises. It is said of the old saints that they, "through faith obtained promises." There would seem to be in prayer the capacity for going even beyond the Word, of getting even beyond His promise, into the very presence of God Himself.

Jacob wrestled not so much with a promise as with the Promiser. We must take hold of the Promiser, lest the promise prove nugatory. Prayer may well be defined as that force which vitalizes and energizes the Word of God by taking hold of God Himself. By taking hold of the Promiser, prayer reissues and makes personal the promise. "There is none . . . that stirreth up himself to take hold of thee [me]," is God's sad lament (Isa. 64:7). "Let him take hold of my strength, that he may make peace with me" (Isa. 27:5), is God's recipe for prayer.

By scriptural warrant, prayer may be divided into the petition of faith and that of submission. The prayer of faith is based on the written Word, for "faith cometh by hearing, and hearing by the Word of God." It receives its answer, inevitably—the very thing for which it prays.

The prayer of submission is without a definite word of promise, so to speak, but takes hold of God with a lowly and contrite spirit and asks and pleads with Him for that which the soul desires. Abraham had no definite promise that God would spare Sodom. Moses had no definite promise that God would spare Israel; on the contrary, there was the declaration of His wrath and of His purpose to destroy. But the devoted leader gained his plea with God when he interceded for the Israelites with incessant prayers and many tears. Daniel had no definite promise that God would reveal to him the meaning of the king's dream, but he prayed specifically, and God answered definitely.

The Word of God is made effectual and operative, by the process and practice of prayer. The Word of the Lord came to Elijah, "Go, shew thyself unto Ahab; and I will send rain upon the earth" (I Kings 18:1). Elijah showed himself to Ahab; but the answer to his prayer did not come until he had pressed his fiery prayer upon the Lord seven times.

Paul had the definite promise from Christ, that he "would be delivered from the people and the Gentiles," but we find him exhorting the Romans in the urgent and solemn manner concerning this very matter:

> Now I beseech you, brethren, for the Lord Jesus Christ's sake, and for the love of the Spirit, that ye strive together with me in your prayers to God for me; That I may be delivered from them that do not believe in Judaea; and that my service which I have for Jerusalem may be accepted of the saints (Rom. 15:30, 31).

The Word of God is a great help in prayer. If it be lodged and written in our hearts, it will form an outflowing current of prayer, full and irresistible. Promises, stored in the heart, are to be the fuel from which prayer receives life and warmth, just as the coal, stored in the earth, ministers to our comfort on stormy days and wintry nights. The Word of God is the food by which prayer is nourished and made strong. Prayer, like man, cannot live by bread alone, "but by every word which proceedeth out of the mouth of the Lord."

Unless the vital forces of prayer are supplied by God's Word, prayer, though earnest, even vociferous, in its urgency, is, in reality, flabby, and vapid, and void. The absence of vital force in praying can be traced to the absence of a constant supply of God's Word to repair the waste and renew the life. He who would learn to pray well must first study God's Word and store it in his memory and thought.

When we consult God's Word, we find that no duty is more binding, more exacting, than that of prayer. On the other hand, we discover that no privilege is more exalted, no habit more richly owned of God. No promises are more radiant, more abounding, more explicit, more often reiterated, than those which are attached to prayer. "All things whatsoever" are received by prayer, because "all things whatsoever" are promised. There is no limit to the provisions included in the promises to prayer and no exclusion from its promises. "Every one that asketh, receiveth." The word of our Lord is to this all-embracing effect: "If ye shall ask any thing in my name, I will do it" (John 14:14).

Here are some of the comprehensive and exhaustive statements of the Word of God *about* prayer, the things to be taken in *by* prayer, the strong promise made in answer *to* prayer:

> "Pray without ceasing"; "continue in prayer"; "continuing instant in prayer"; "in everything by prayer, let your request be made known unto God"; "pray always, pray and not faint"; "men should pray everywhere"; "praying always, with all prayer and supplication."

What clear and strong statements are those which are put in the divine record, to furnish us with a sure basis of faith, and to urge, constrain, and encourage us to pray! How wide the range of prayer as given us in the divine revelation! How these Scriptures incite us to seek the God of prayer with all our wants, with all our burdens!

In addition to these statements left on record for our encouragement, the sacred pages teem with facts, examples, incidents, and observations, stressing the importance and the absolute necessity of prayer and putting emphasis on its all-prevailing power.

The utmost reach and full benefit of the rich promises of the Word of God should humbly be received by us and put to the test. The world will never receive the full benefits of the gospel until this be done. Neither Christian experience nor Christian living will be what they ought to be till these divine promises have been fully tested by those who pray. By prayer, we bring these promises of God's holy will into the realm of the actual and the real. Prayer is the philosopher's stone which transmutes them into gold.

If it be asked what is to be done in order to render God's promises real, the answer is that we must *pray* until the words of the promise are clothed upon with the rich raiment of fulfillment.

God's promises are altogether too large to be mastered by desultory praying. When we examine ourselves, all too often we discover that our praying does not rise to the demands of the situation; is so limited that it is little more than a mere oasis amid the waste and desert of the world's sin. Who of us, in our praying, measures up to this promise of our Lord:

> Verily, verily, I say unto you, he that believeth on me, the works that I do shall he do also; and greater works than these shall he do; because I go unto my Father (John 14:12).

How comprehensive, how far reaching, how all-embracing! How much is here for the glory of God, how much for the good of man! How much for the manifestation of Christ's enthroned power, how much for the reward of abundant faith! And how great and gracious are the results which can be made to accrue from the exercise of commensurate, believing prayer!

Look for a moment at another of God's great promises and discover how we may be undergirded by the Word as we pray and on what firm ground we may stand on which to make our petitions to our God:

> If ye abide in me, and my words abide in you, ye shall ask what ye will, and it shall be done unto you (John 15:7).

In these comprehensive words God turns Himself over to the will of His people. When Christ becomes our all-in-all, prayer lays God's treasures at our feet. Primitive Christianity had an easy and practical solution of the situation, and got all which God had to give. That simple and terse solution is recorded in John's First Epistle:

> And whatsoever we ask, we receive of him, because we keep his commandments, and do those things that are pleasing in his sight (I John 3:22).

Prayer, coupled with loving obedience, is the way to put God to the test and to make prayer answer all ends and all things. Prayer, joined to the Word of God, hallows and makes sacred all God's gifts. Prayer is not simply to get things from God, but to make those things holy which already have been received from Him. It is not merely to get a blessing, but also to be able to give a blessing. Prayer makes common things holy and secular things sacred. It receives things from God with thanksgiving and hallows them with thankful hearts and devoted service.

In the First Epistle to Timothy, Paul gives us these words:

> For every creature of God is good, and nothing to be refused, if it be received with thanksgiving: For it is sanctified by the word of God and prayer (I Tim. 4:4, 5).

That is a statement which gives a negative to mere asceticism. God's good gifts are to be holy not only by God's creative power, but also because they are made holy to us by prayer. We receive them, appropriate them, and sanctify them by prayer.

Doing God's will, and having His Word abiding in us, is an imperative of effectual praying. But, it may be asked, how are we to know what God's will is? The answer is, by studying His Word, by hiding it in our hearts, and by letting the Word dwell in us richly. "The entrance of thy word, giveth light."

To know God's will in prayer, we must be filled with God's Spirit, who maketh intercession for the saints and in the saints, according to the will of God. To be filled with God's Spirit, to be filled with God's Word, is to know God's will. It is to be put in such a frame of mind, to be found in such a state of heart, as will enable us to read and interpret aright the purposes of the Infinite. Such filling of the heart with the Word and the Spirit gives us an insight into the will of the Father, enables us to rightly discern His will, and puts within us a disposition of mind and heart to make it the guide and compass of our lives.

Epaphras prayed that the Colossians might stand "perfect and complete in all the will of God." This is proof positive that not only may we know the will of God, but that we may know *all* the will of God. And not only may we know all the will of God, but we may *do* all the will of God. We may, moreover, do all the will of God, not occasionally or by a mere impulse, but with a settled habit of conduct. Still further, it shows us that we may not only do the will of God externally, but from the heart, doing it cheerfully, without reluctance, or secret disinclination, or any drawing or holding back from the intimate presence of the Lord.

Some years ago a man was travelling in the wilds of Kentucky. He had with him a large sum of money and was well armed. He put up at a log-house one night, but was much concerned with the rough appearance of the men who came and went from this abode. He retired early but not to sleep. At midnight he heard the dogs barking furiously and the sound of someone entering the cabin. Peering through a chink in the boards of his room, he saw a stranger with a gun in his hand. Another man sat before the fire. The traveller concluded they were planning to rob him, and prepared to defend himself and his property. Presently the newcomer took down a copy of the Bible, read a chapter aloud, and then knelt down and prayed. The traveller dismissed his fears, put his revolver away and lay down, to sleep peacefully until morning light. And all because a Bible was in the cabin, and its owner a man of prayer.—F. F. Shoup

Prayer has all to do with the success of the preaching of the Word. This Paul clearly teaches in that familiar and pressing request he made to the Thessalonians:

> Finally, brethren, pray for us, that the Word of the Lord may have free course, and be glorified ... (II Thess. 3:3).

Prayer opens the way for the Word of God to run without let or hindrance and creates the atmosphere which is favorable to the Word accomplishing its purpose. Prayer puts wheels under God's Word and gives wings to the angel of the Lord, "having the everlasting gospel to preach unto them that dwell on the earth, and to every nation, and kindred, and tongue, and people" (Rev. 14:6). Prayer greatly helps the Word of the Lord.

The Parable of the Sower is a notable study of preaching, showing its differing effects and describing the diversity of hearers. The wayside hearers are legion. The soil lies all unprepared either by previous thought or prayer; as a consequence, the devil easily takes away the seed (which is the Word of God) and dissipating all good impressions, renders the work of the sower futile. No one for a moment believes that so much of present-day sowing would go fruitless if only the hearers would prepare the ground of their hearts beforehand by prayer and meditation.

Similarly with the stony-ground hearers, and the thorny-ground hearers: although the word lodges in their hearts and begins to sprout, yet all is lost, chiefly because there is no prayer or watchfulness or cultivation following. The good-ground hearers are profited by the sowing, simply because their minds have been prepared for the reception of the seed, and that, after hearing, they have cultivated the seed sown in their hearts, by the exercise of prayer. All this gives peculiar emphasis to the conclusion of this striking parable: "Take heed, therefore, how ye hear." And in order that we *may* take heed how we hear, it is needful to give ourselves continually to prayer.

We have *got* to believe that underlying God's Word is prayer, and upon prayer its final success will depend. In the Book of Isaiah we read:

So shall my word be that goeth forth out of my mouth: it shall not return unto me void, but it shall accomplish that which I please, and it shall prosper in the thing whereto I sent it (Isa. 55:11).

In Psalm 19, David magnifies the Word of God in six statements concerning it. It converts the soul, makes wise the simple, rejoices the heart, enlightens the eyes, endures eternally, and is true and righteous altogether. The Word of God is perfect, sure, right, pure. It is heart-searching, and, at the same time, purifying in its effect. It is no surprise therefore that after considering the deep spirituality of the Word of God, its power to search the inner nature of man, and its deep purity, the psalmist should close his dissertation with this passage:

> "Who can understand his errors?" And then praying after this fashion: "cleanse thou me from secret faults. Keep back thy servant also from presumptuous sins; let them not have dominion over me. ... Let the words of my mouth, and the meditation of my heart, be acceptable in thy sight, O Lord, my strength, and my redeemer" (Ps. 19:12-14).

James recognizes the deep spirituality of the Word, and its inherent saving power, in the following ex-hortation:

> Wherefore, lay apart all filthiness and superfluity of naughtiness, and receive with meekness the engrafted word, which is able to save your souls (James 1:21).

And Peter talks along the same line when describing the saving power of the Word of God:

> Being born again, not of corruptible seed, but of incor-ruptible, by the word of God, which liveth and abideth for ever (I Peter 1:23).

Not only does Peter speak of being born again, by the incorruptible Word of God, but he informs us that to grow in grace we must be like newborn babes, desiring or feeding upon the "sincere milk of the Word."

That is not to say, however, that the mere form of

words as they occur in the Bible have in them any saving efficacy. But the Word of God, be it remembered, is impregnated with the Holy Spirit. And just as there is a divine element in the words of Scripture, so also is the same divine element to be found in all true preaching of the Word which is able to save and convert the soul.

Prayer invariably begets a love for the Word of God, and sets people to the reading of it. Prayer leads people to obey the Word of God, and puts into the heart which obeys a joy unspeakable. Praying people and Bible-reading people are the same sort of folk. The God of the Bible and the God of prayer are one. God speaks to man in the Bible; man speaks to God in prayer. One reads the Bible to discover God's will; he prays in order that he may receive power to do that will. Bible reading and praying are the distinguishing traits of those who strive to know and please God. And just as prayer begets a love for the Scriptures and sets people to reading the Bible, so, also, does prayer cause men and women to visit the house of God to hear the Scriptures expounded. Church going is closely connected with the Bible, not so much because the Bible cautions us against "forsaking the assembling of ourselves together as the manner of some is," but because in God's house God's chosen minister declares His Word to dying men, explains the Scriptures, and enforces their teachings upon his hearers. And prayer germinates a resolve in those who practice it not to forsake the house of God.

Prayer begets a church-going conscience, a church-loving heart, a church-supporting spirit. It is the praying people, who make it a matter of conscience, to attend the preaching of the Word; who delight in its reading; exposition; who support it with their influence and their means. Prayer exalts the Word of God and gives it preeminence in the estimation of those who faithfully and wholeheartedly call upon the name of the Lord.

Prayer draws its very life from the Bible, and has no standing ground outside of the warrant of the Scriptures. Its very existence and character is dependent on revelation made by God to man in His Holy Word. Prayer, in turn, exalts this same revelation and turns men toward that Word. The nature, necessity, and all-comprehending character of prayer is based on the Word of God.

Psalm 119 is a directory of God's Word. With three or four exceptions, each verse contains a word which identifies or locates the Word of God. Quite often the writer breaks out into supplication, several times praying, "Teach me thy statutes." So deeply impressed is he with the wonders of God's Word and of the need for divine illumination wherewith to see and understand the wonderful things recorded therein that he fervently prays:

> Open thou mine eyes, that I may behold wondrous things out of thy law (Ps. 119:18).

From the opening of this wonderful Psalm to its close, prayer and God's Word are intertwined. Almost every phase of God's Word is touched upon by this inspired writer. So thoroughly convinced was the psalmist of the deep spiritual power of the Word of God that he makes this declaration:

> Thy word have I hid in mine heart, that I might not sin against thee (Ps. 119:11).

Here the psalmist found his protection against sinning. By having God's Word hidden in his heart; in having his whole being thoroughly impregnated with that Word; in being brought completely under its benign and gracious influence, he was enabled to walk to and fro in the earth, safe from the attack of the evil one and for-tified against a proneness to wander out of the way.

We find, furthermore, the power of prayer to create a real love for the Scriptures and to put within men a nature which will take pleasure in the Word. In holy ecstasy he cries, "O how love I thy law! it is my medi-tation all the day" (Ps. 119:97). And again: "How sweet are thy words unto my taste! yea, sweeter than honey to my mouth" (Ps. 119:103).

Would we have a relish for God's Word? Then let us give ourselves continually to prayer. He who would have a heart for the reading of the Bible must not — dare not — forget to pray. The man of whom it can be said, "His delight is in the law of the Lord," is the man who can truly say, "I delight to visit the place of prayer." No man loves the Bible who does not love to pray. No man loves to pray who does not delight in the law of the Lord.

Our Lord was a man of prayer and He magnified the Word of God, quoting often from the Scriptures. Right through His earthly life Jesus observed Sabbath keeping, church going, and the reading of the Word of God, and had prayer intermingled with them all:

And he came to Nazareth, where he had been brought up: and, as his custom was, he went into the synagogue on the sabbath day, and stood up for to read (Luke 4:16).

Here, let it be said, that no two things are more es-sential to a spirit-filled life than Bible reading and secret prayer; no two things more helpful to growth in grace; to getting the largest joy out of a Christian life; toward establishing one in the ways of eternal peace. The ne-glect of these all-important duties presages leanness of soul, loss of joy, absence of peace, dryness of spirit, decay in all that pertains to spiritual life. Neglecting these things paves the way for apostasy, and gives the evil one an advantage such as he is not likely to ignore. Reading God's Word regularly and praying habitually in the secret place of the Most High puts one where he is absolutely safe from the attacks of the enemy of souls and guarantees him salvation and final victory through the overcoming power of the Lamb.

2

Prayer and Faith

A dear friend of mine who was quite a lover of the chase, told me the following story: "Rising early one morning," he said, "I heard the baying of a score of deerhounds in pursuit of their quarry. Looking away to a broad, open field in front of me, I saw a young fawn making its way across, and giving signs, moreover, that its race was well-nigh run. Reaching the rails of the enclosure, it leaped over and crouched within ten feet from where I stood. A moment later two of the hounds came over, when the fawn ran in my direction and pushed its head between my legs. I lifted the little thing to my breast, and, swinging round and round, fought off the dogs. I felt, just then, that all the dogs in the West could not, and should not capture that fawn after its weakness had appealed to my strength." So is it, when human helplessness appeals to Almighty God. Well do I remember when the hounds of sin were after my soul, until, at last, I ran into the arms of Almighty God.—A. C. Dixon

In any study of the principles and procedure of prayer, of its activities and enterprises, first place must, of necessity, be given to faith. It is the initial quality in the heart of any man who essays to talk to the unseen. He must, out of sheer helplessness, stretch forth hands of faith. He *must* believe where he cannot prove. In the ultimate issue, prayer is simply faith claiming its natural yet marvelous prerogatives — faith taking possession of its illimitable inheritance. True godliness is just as true, steady, and persevering in the realm of faith as it is in the province of prayer. Moreover: when faith ceases to pray, it ceases to live.

Faith does the impossible because it brings God to undertake for us, and nothing is impossible with God. How great — without qualification or limitation — is the power of faith! If doubt be banished from the heart, and unbelief made stranger there, what we ask of God shall surely come to pass, and a believer hath vouchsafed to him "whatsoever he saith."

Prayer projects faith on God, and God on the world. Only God can move mountains, but faith and prayer move God. In His cursing of the fig tree our Lord demonstrated His power. Following that, He proceeded to declare that large powers were committed to faith and prayer, not in order to kill but to make alive, not to blast but to bless.

At this point in our study, we turn to a saying of our Lord which there is need to emphasize since it is the very keystone of the arch of faith and prayer.

> Therefore I say unto you, What things soever ye desire, when ye pray, believe that ye receive them, and ye shall have them (Mark 11:24).

We should ponder well that statement — "Believe that ye receive them, and ye shall have them." Here is described a faith which realizes, which appropriates, which *takes*. Such faith is a consciousness of the divine, an experienced communion, a realized certainty.

Is faith growing or declining as the years go by? Does faith stand strong and foursquare these days as iniquity abounds and the love of many grows cold? Does faith maintain its hold as religion tends to become a mere formality and worldliness increasingly prevails? The enquiry of our Lord may, with great appropriateness, be ours. "When the Son of man cometh," He asks, "shall he find faith on the earth?" We believe that He will, and it is ours, in this our day, to see to it that the lamp of faith is trimmed and burning, lest He come who *shall* come, and that right early.

Faith is the foundation of Christian character and the security of the soul. When Jesus was looking forward to Peter's denial and cautioning him against it, He said unto His disciple:

> Simon, Simon, behold, Satan hath desired to have you, that he may sift you as wheat: But I have prayed for thee, that thy faith fail not... (Luke 22:31, 32).

Our Lord was declaring a central truth. It was Peter's faith He was seeking to guard, for well He knew that when faith is broken down, the foundations of spiritual life give way and the entire structure of religious experience falls. It was Peter's faith which needed guarding. Hence Christ's solicitude for the welfare of His disciples's soul and His determination to fortify Peter's faith by His own all-prevailing prayer.

In his Second Epistle Peter has this idea in mind when speaking of growth in grace as a measure of safety in the Christian life, and as implying fruitfulness.

> And beside this, giving diligence, add to your faith virtue; and to virtue knowledge; and to knowledge tem-

perance; and to temperance patience; and to patience
godliness (II Peter 1:5, 6).

Of this additioning process, faith was the starting-
point—the basis of the other graces of the Spirit. Faith
was the foundation on which other things were to be
built. Peter does not enjoin his readers to add to works
or gifts or virtues but to *faith*. Much depends on starting
right in this business of growing in grace. There is a
divine order of which Peter was aware; and so he goes
on to declare that we are to give diligence to making
our calling and election sure, which election is rendered
certain adding to faith which, in turn, is done by constant, earnest praying. Thus faith is kept alive by prayer,
and every step taken in this adding of grace to grace is
accompanied by prayer.

The faith which creates powerful praying is the faith
which centers itself on a powerful person. Faith in Christ's
ability to *do* and to do *greatly* is the faith which prays
greatly. Thus the leper lay hold upon the power of Christ.
"Lord, if thou wilt," he cried, "thou canst make me clean."
In this instance we are shown how faith centered in
Christ's ability to *do*, and how it secured the healing
power.

It was concerning this very point that Jesus questioned the blind men who came to Him for healing:

"Believe ye that I am able to do this?" They said unto
him, "Yea, Lord." Then touched he their eyes, saying,
"According to your faith be it unto you" (Matt. 9:28, 29).

It was to inspire faith in His ability to *do* that Jesus
left behind Him that last, great statement, which, in the
final analysis, is a ringing challenge to faith. "All power,"
He declared, "is given unto me in heaven and in earth."

Again: faith is obedient; it goes when commanded, as did the nobleman who came to Jesus in the day of His flesh, and whose son was grievously sick.

Moreover: such faith acts. Like the man who was born blind, it goes to wash in the pool of Siloam when *told* to wash. Like Peter on Gennesaret it casts the net where Jesus commands, instantly, without question or doubt. Such faith takes away the stone from the grave of Lazarus promptly. A praying faith keeps the commandments of God and does those things which are well pleasing in His sight. It asks, "Lord, what wilt thou have me to do?" and answers quickly, "Speak, Lord, thy servant heareth." Obedience helps faith, and faith, in turn, helps obedience. To do God's will is essential to true faith, and faith is necessary to implicit obedience.

Yet faith is called upon, and that right often, to wait in patience before God and is prepared for God's seeming delays in answering prayer. Faith does not grow disheartened because prayer is not immediately honored; it takes God at His Word and lets Him take what time He chooses in fulfilling His purposes and in carrying on His work. There is bound to be much delay and long days of waiting for true faith, but faith accepts the conditions—knows there will be delays in answering prayer and regards such delays as times of testing, in the which it is privileged to show its mettle and the stern stuff of which it is made.

The case of Lazarus was an instance of where there was delay, where the faith of two good women was sorely tried: Lazarus was critically ill, and his sisters sent for Jesus. But without any known reason, our Lord delayed His going to the relief of His sick friend. The plea was urgent and touching—"Lord, behold, he whom thou lovest is sick,"—but the Master was not moved by it, and the women's earnest request seemed to fall on deaf ears. What a trial to faith! Furthermore: our Lord's tardiness appeared to bring about hopeless disaster. While Jesus tarried, Lazarus died.

But the delay of Jesus was exercised in the interests of a greater good. Finally, He made His way to the home in Bethany.

> Then said Jesus unto them plainly, "Lazarus is dead. And I am glad for your sakes that I was not there, to the intent ye may believe; nevertheless let us go unto him" (John 11:14).

Fear not, O tempted and tried believer; Jesus *will* come if patience be exercised and faith hold fast. His delay will serve to make His coming the more richly blessed. Pray on. Wait on. Thou canst not fail. If Christ delay, wait for Him. In His own good time, He *will* come, and will not tarry.

Delay is often the test and the strength of faith. How much patience is required when these times of testing come! Yet faith gathers strength by waiting and praying. Patience has its perfect work in the school of delay. In some instances, delay is of the very essence of the prayer. God has to do many things antecedent to giving the final answer — things which are essential to the lasting good of him who is requesting favor at His hands.

Jacob prayed, with point and ardor, to be delivered from Esau. But before that prayer could be answered, there was much to be done with and for Jacob. He must be changed, as well as Esau. Jacob had to be made into a new man before Esau could be. Jacob had to be converted to God before Esau could be converted to Jacob.

Among the large and luminous utterances of Jesus concerning prayer none is more arresting than this:

Verily, verily, I say unto you, He that believeth on me, the works that I do shall he do also; and greater works than these shall he do; because I go unto my Father. And whatsoever ye shall ask in my name, that will I do, that the Father may be glorified in the Son. If ye shall ask anything in my name, I will do it (John 14:12, 13).

How wonderful are these statements of what God will do in answer to prayer! Of how great importance these ringing words, prefaced as they are with the most solemn verity! Faith in Christ is the basis of all working and of all praying. All wonderful works depend on wonderful praying, and all praying is done in the name of Jesus Christ. Amazing lesson, of wondrous simplicity, is this praying in the name of the Lord Jesus! All other conditions are depreciated, everything else is renounced, save Jesus only. The name of Christ — the person of our Lord and Savior Jesus Christ — must be supremely sovereign, in the hour and article of prayer.

If Jesus dwell at the fountain of my life; if the currents of His life have displaced and superseded all self-currents; if implicit obedience to Him be the inspiration and force of every movement of my life, then He can safely commit the praying to my will, and pledge Himself, by an obligation as profound as His own nature, that whatsoever is asked shall be granted. Nothing can be clearer, more distinct, more unlimited both in application and extent, than the exhortation and urgency of Christ, "Have faith in God."

Faith covers temporal as well as spiritual needs. Faith dispels all undue anxiety and needless care about what shall be eaten, what shall be drunk, what shall be worn. Faith lives in the present, and regards the day as being sufficient unto the evil thereof. It lives day by day and dispels all fears for the morrow. Faith brings great ease of mind and perfect peace of heart.

Thou wilt keep him in perfect peace, whose mind is stayed on thee: because he trusteth in thee (Isa. 26:3).

When we pray, "Give us this day our daily bread," we are, in a measure, shutting tomorrow out of our prayer. We do not live in tomorrow but in today. We do not seek tomorrow's grace or tomorrow's bread. They thrive best, and get most out of life, who live in the living present. They pray best who pray for today's needs, not for tomorrow's, which may render our prayers unnecessary and redundant by not existing at all!

True prayers are born of present trials and present needs. Bread for today is bread enough. Bread given for today is the strongest sort of pledge that there will be bread tomorrow. Victory today is the assurance of victory tomorrow. Our prayers need to be focused upon the present. We must trust God today, and leave the morrow entirely with Him. The present is ours; the future belongs to God. Prayer is the task and duty of each recurring day—daily prayer for daily needs.

As every day demands its bread, so every day demands its prayer. No amount of praying done today will suffice for tomorrow's praying. On the other hand, no praying for tomorrow is of any great value to us today. Today's manna is what we need; tomorrow God will see that our needs are supplied. This is the faith which God seeks to inspire. So leave tomorrow, with its cares, its needs, its troubles, in God's hands. There is no storing tomorrow's grace or tomorrow's praying; neither is there any laying up of today's grace to meet tomorrow's necessities. We cannot have tomorrow's grace, we cannot eat tomorrow's bread, we cannot do tomorrow's praying. "Sufficient unto the day is the evil thereof;" and, most assuredly, if we possess faith, sufficient also will be the good.

The guests at a certain hotel were being rendered uncomfortable by repeated strumming on a piano, done by a little girl who possessed no knowledge of music. They complained to the proprietor with a view to having the annoyance stopped. "I am sorry you are annoyed," he said. "But the girl is the child of one of my very best guests. I can scarcely ask her not to touch the piano. But her father, who is away for a day or so, will return tomorrow. You can then approach him, and have the matter set right." When the father returned, he found his daughter in the reception-room and, as usual, thumping on the piano. He walked up behind the child and, putting his arms over her shoulders, took her hands in his, and produced some most beautiful music. Thus it may be with us, and thus it will be, some coming day. Just now, we can produce little but clamour and disharmony; but, one day, the Lord Jesus will take hold of our hands of faith and prayer, and use them to bring forth the music of the skies. — Anon.

Genuine, authentic faith must be definite and free of doubt. Not simply general in character; not a mere belief in the being, goodness, and power of God, but a faith which believes that the things which "he saith, shall come to pass." As the faith is specific, so the answer likewise will be definite: "He shall have whatsoever he saith." Faith and prayer select the things, and God commits Himself to do the very things which faith and persevering prayer nominate and petition Him to accomplish.

The American Revised Version renders the twenty-fourth verse of the eleventh chapter of Mark thus: "Therefore I say unto you, All things whatsoever ye pray and ask for, believe that ye receive them, and ye shall have them." Perfect faith has always in its keeping what perfect prayer asks for. How large and unqualified is the area of operation—the "All things whatsoever!" How definite and specific the promise—"Ye shall have them!"

Our chief concern is with our faith—the problems of its growth and the activities of its vigorous maturity. A faith which grasps and holds in its keeping the very things it asks for, without wavering, doubt or fear—that is the faith we need—faith, such as is a pearl of great price, in the process and practice of prayer.

The statement of our Lord about faith and prayer quoted above is of supreme importance. Faith must be definite, specific; an unqualified, unmistakable request for the things asked for. It is not to be a vague, indefinite, shadowy thing; it must be something more than an abstract belief in God's willingness and ability to do for us. It is to be a definite, specific, asking for, and expecting the things for which we ask. Note the reading of Mark 11:23:

> ... and shall not doubt in his heart, but shall believe that those things which he saith shall come to pass; he shall have whatsoever he saith.

Just so far as the faith and the asking is definite, so also will the answer be. The giving is not to be something other than the things prayed for, but the actual things sought and named. "He shall have whatsoever he saith." It is all imperative, "He shall have." The granting is to be unlimited, both in quality and in quantity.

Faith and prayer select the subjects for petition, thereby determining what God is to do. "He shall have whatsoever he saith." Christ holds Himself ready to supply exactly and fully all the demands of faith and prayer. If the order on God be made clear, specific, and definite, God will fill it, exactly in accordance with the presented terms.

Faith is not an abstract belief in the Word of God, nor a mere mental credence, nor a simple assent of the understanding and will; nor is it a passive acceptance of facts, however sacred or thorough. Faith is an operation of God, a divine illumination, a holy energy implanted by the Word of God and the Spirit in the human soul — a spiritual, divine principle which takes of the supernatural and makes it a thing apprehendable by the faculties of time and sense.

Faith deals with God and is conscious of God. It deals with the Lord Jesus Christ and sees in Him a Savior; it deals with God's Word and lays hold of the truth; it deals with the Spirit of God and is energized and inspired by its holy fire. God is the great objective of faith; for faith rests its whole weight on His Word. Faith is not an aimless act of the soul but a looking to God and a resting upon His promises. Just as love and hope have always an objective so, also, has faith. Faith is not believing just *anything*; it is believing God, resting in Him, trusting His Word.

Faith gives birth to prayer and grows stronger, strikes deeper, rises higher, in the struggles and wrestlings of mighty petitioning. Faith is the substance of things hoped for, the assurance and realization of the inheritance of the saints. Faith, too, is humble and persevering. It can wait and pray; it can stay on its knees or lie in the dust. It is the one great condition of prayer; the lack of it lies at the root of all poor praying, feeble praying, little praying, unanswered praying.

The nature and meaning of faith is more demonstrable in what it does than it is by reason of any definition given it. Thus, if we turn to the record of faith given us in that great honor roll, which constitutes the eleventh chapter of Hebrews, we see something of the

wonderful results of faith. What a glorious list it is—
that of these men and women of faith! What marvelous
achievements are there recorded and set to the credit of
faith! The inspired writer, exhausting his resources in
cataloguing the Old Testament saints who were such
notable examples of wonderful faith, finally exclaims:

> And what shall I more say? for the time would fail me
> to tell of Gedeon, and of Barak, and of Samson, and of
> Jephthae; of David also, and Samuel, and of the prophets
> (Heb. 11:32).

And then the writer of Hebrews goes on again, in a
wonderful strain, telling of the unrecorded exploits
wrought through the faith of the men of old, "of whom
the world was not worthy." "All these," he says, "obtained a good report through faith."

What an era of glorious achievements would dawn
for the church and the world if only there could be reproduced a race of saints of like mighty faith, of like
wonderful praying! It is not the intellectually great that
the church needs, nor is it men of wealth that the times
demand. It is not people of great social influence that
this day requires. Above everybody and everything else,
it is men of faith, men of mighty prayer, men and women
after the fashion of the saints and heroes enumerated in
Hebrews, who "obtained a good report through faith,"
that the church and the whole wide world of humanity
needs.

Many men of this day obtain a good report because
of their money giving, their great mental gifts and talents, but few there be who obtain a "good report" because of their great faith in God, or because of the
wonderful things which are being wrought through their

great praying. Today, as much as at any time, we need men of great faith and men who are great in prayer. These are the two cardinal virtues which make men great in the eyes of God, the two things which create conditions of real spiritual success in the life and work of the church. It is our chief concern to see that we maintain a faith of such quality and texture as counts before God; which grasps and holds in its keeping the things for which it asks without doubt and without fear.

Doubt and fear are the twin foes of faith. Sometimes they actually usurp the place of faith, and although we pray it is a restless, disquieted prayer that we offer, uneasy and often complaining. Peter failed to walk on Gennesaret because he permitted the waves to break over him and swamp the power of his faith. Taking his eyes from the Lord and regarding the water all about him, he began to sink and had to cry for succor—"Lord, save, or I perish!"

Doubts should never be cherished, nor fears harbored. Let none cherish the delusion that he is a martyr to fear and doubt. It is no credit to any man's mental capacity to cherish doubt of God, and no comfort can possibly derive from such a thought. Our eyes should be taken off self, removed from our own weakness and allowed to rest implicitly upon God's strength. "Cast not away therefore your confidence, which hath great recompence of reward." A simple, confiding faith, living day by day, and casting its burden on the Lord each hour of the day, will dissipate fear, drive away misgiving, and deliver from doubt:

Be careful for nothing; but in every thing by prayer and supplication with thanksgiving let your requests be made known unto God (Phil. 4:6).

That is the divine cure for all fear, anxiety, and undue concern of soul, all of which are closely akin to doubt and unbelief. This is the divine prescription for securing the peace which passeth all understanding and keeps the heart and mind in quietness and peace.

All of us need to mark well and heed the caution given in Hebrews 3:12: "Take heed, brethren, lest there be in any of you an evil heart of unbelief, in departing from the living God."

We need also to guard against unbelief as we would against an enemy. Faith needs to be cultivated. We need to keep on praying, "Lord, increase our faith," for faith is susceptible of increase. Paul's tribute to the Thessalonians was that their faith grew exceedingly. Faith is increased by exercise, by being put into use. It is nourished by sore trials.

> That the trial of your faith, being much more precious than of gold that perisheth, though it be tried with fire, might be found unto praise and honour and glory at the appearing of Jesus Christ (I Peter 1:7).

Faith grows by reading and meditating upon the Word of God. Most, and best of all, faith thrives in an atmosphere of prayer.

It would be well if all of us were to stop and inquire personally of ourselves: "Have I faith in God? Have I *real* faith — faith which keeps me in perfect peace about the things of earth and the things of heaven?" This is the most important question a man can propound and expect to be answered. And there is another question, closely akin to it in significance and importance — "Do I really pray to God so that He hears me and answers my prayers? And do I truly pray unto God so that I get direct from God the things I ask of Him?"

It was claimed for Augustus Caesar that he found Rome a city of wood, and left it a city of marble. The pastor who succeeds in changing his people from a prayerless to a prayerful people has done a greater work than did Augustus in changing a city from wood to marble. And after all, this is the prime work of the preacher. Primarily, he is dealing with prayerless people — with people of whom it is said, "God is not in all their thoughts." Such people he meets everywhere and all the time. His main business is to turn them from being forgetful of God, from being devoid of faith, from being prayerless, so that they become people who habitually pray, who believe in God, remember Him, and do His will. The preacher is not sent to merely induce men to join the church, nor merely to get them to do better. It is to get them to pray, to trust God, and to keep God ever before their eyes that they may not sin against Him.

The work of the ministry is to change unbelieving sinners into praying and believing saints. The call goes forth by divine authority, "Believe on the Lord Jesus Christ, and thou shalt be saved." We catch a glimpse of the tremendous importance of faith and of the great value God has set upon it when we remember that He has made it the one indispensable condition of being saved. "By grace are ye saved, through faith." Thus, when we contemplate the great importance of prayer, we find faith standing immediately by its side. By faith are we saved, and by faith we *stay* saved. Prayer introduces us to a life of faith. Paul declared that the life he lived, he lived by faith in the Son of God who loved him and gave Himself for him — that he walked by faith and not by sight.

Prayer is absolutely dependent upon faith. Virtually, it has no existence apart from it, and accomplishes nothing unless it be its inseparable companion. Faith makes prayer effectual and in a certain important sense must precede it.

> ... for he that cometh to God must believe that he is, and that he is a rewarder of them that diligently seek him (Heb. 11:6).

Before prayer ever starts toward God; before its petition is preferred, before its requests are made known — faith must have gone on ahead; must have asserted its belief in the existence of God; must have given its assent to the gracious truth that "God is a rewarder of those that diligently seek His face." This is the primary step in praying. In this regard, while faith does not bring the blessing, yet it puts prayer in a position to ask for it, and leads to another step toward realization, by aiding the petitioner to believe that God is able and willing to bless.

Faith starts prayer to work — clears the way to the mercy seat. It gives assurance, first of all, that there is a mercy seat, and that there the High Priest awaits the pray-ers and the prayers. Faith opens the way for prayer to approach God. But it does more. It accompanies prayer at every step she takes. It is her inseparable companion, and when requests are made unto God, it is faith which turns the asking into obtaining. And faith follows prayer, since the spiritual life into which a believer is led by prayer is a life of faith. The one prominent characteristic of the experience into which believers are brought through prayer is not a life of works, but of faith.

Faith makes prayer strong and gives it patience to wait on God. Faith believes that God is a rewarder. No truth is more clearly revealed in the Scriptures than this, while none is more encouraging. Even the closet has its promised reward, "He that seeth in secret, shall reward thee openly," while the most insignificant service rendered to a disciple in the name of the Lord surely receives its reward. And to this precious truth faith gives its hearty assent.

Yet faith is narrowed down to one particular thing—it does not believe that God will reward everybody, nor that He is a rewarder of all who pray, but that He is a rewarder of them that *diligently seek Him*. Faith rests its case on diligence in prayer and gives assurance and encouragement to diligent seekers after God, for it is they, alone, who are richly rewarded when they pray.

We need constantly to be reminded that faith is the one inseparable condition of successful praying. There are other considerations entering into the exercise, but faith is the final, the one indispensable condition of true praying. As it is written in a familiar, primary declaration: "Without faith, it is impossible to please Him."

James puts this truth very plainly.

> If any of you lack wisdom, let him ask of God, that giveth to all men liberally, and upbraideth not; and it shall be given him. But let him ask in faith, nothing wavering. For he that wavereth [or doubteth] is like a wave of the sea driven with the wind and tossed. For let not that man think that he shall receive any thing of the Lord (James 1:5-7).

Doubting is always put under the ban because it stands as a foe to faith and hinders effectual praying. In the First Epistle to Timothy Paul gives us an invaluable truth relative to the conditions of successful praying, which he thus lays down: "I will therefore that men pray every where, lifting up holy hands, without wrath and doubting" (2:8).

All questioning must be watched against and eschewed. Fear and peradventure have no place in true praying. Faith must assert itself and bid these foes to prayer depart.

Too much authority cannot be attributed to faith; but prayer is the scepter by which it signalizes its power. How much of spiritual wisdom there is in the following advice written by an eminent old divine.

Would you be freed from the bondage to corruption? he asks. Would you grow in grace in general and grow in grace in particular? If you would, your way is plain. Ask of God more faith. Beg of Him morning, and noon and night, while you walk by the way, while you sit in the house, when you lie down and when you rise up; beg of Him simply to impress Divine things more deeply on your heart, to give you more and more of the substance of things hoped for and of the evidence of things not seen.

Great incentives to pray are furnished in Holy Scriptures, and our Lord closes His teaching about prayer with the assurance and promise of heaven. The presence of Jesus Christ in heaven, the preparation for His saints which He is making there, and the assurance that He will come again to receive them—how all this helps the weariness of praying, strengthens its conflicts, sweetens its arduous toil! These things are the star of hope to prayer, the wiping away of its tears, the putting of the odor of heaven into the bitterness of its cry. The spirit of a pilgrim greatly facilitates praying. An earthbound, earth-satisfied spirit cannot pray. In such a heart the flame of spiritual desire is either gone out or smoldering in faintest glow. The wings of its faith are clipped, its eyes are filmed, its tongue silenced. But they who in unswerving faith and unceasing prayer wait continually upon the Lord *do* renew their strength, *do* mount up with wings as eagles, *do* run, and are not weary, *do* walk, and not faint.

Excerpts from
The Essentials of Prayer

Prayer and Humility
Prayer and Devotion
Prayer, Praise, and Thanksgiving

3

Prayer and Humility

If two angels were to receive at the same moment a commission from God, one to go down and rule earth's grandest empire, the other to go and sweep the streets of its meanest village, it would be a matter of entire indifference to each which service fell to his lot, the post of ruler or the post of scavenger; for the joy of the angels lies only in obedience to God's will, and with equal joy they would lift a Lazarus in his rags to Abraham's bosom, or be a chariot of fire to carry an Elijah home. — John Newton

To be humble is to have a low estimate of one's self. It is to be modest, lowly, with a disposition to seek obscurity. Humility retires itself from the public gaze. It does not seek publicity nor hunt for high places, neither does it care for prominence. Humility is retiring in its nature. Self-abasement belongs to humility. It is given to self-depreciation. It never exalts itself in the eyes of others nor even in the eyes of itself. Modesty is one of its most prominent characteristics.

In humility there is the total absence of pride, and it is at the very farthest distance from anything like self-conceit. There is no self-praise in humility. Rather it has the disposition to praise others. "In honour preferring one another." It is not given to self-exaltation. Humility does not love the uppermost seats and aspire to the high places. It is willing to take the lowliest seat and prefers those places where it will be unnoticed. The prayer of humility is after this fashion:

> Never let the world break in,
> Fix a mighty gulf between;
> Keep me humble and unknown,
> Prized and loved by God alone.

Humility does not have its eyes on self, but rather on God and others. It is poor in spirit, meek in behavior, lowly in heart. "With all lowliness and meekness, with longsuffering, forbearing one another in love" (Eph. 4:2).

The parable of the Pharisee and publican is a sermon in brief on humility and self-praise. The Pharisee, given over to self-conceit, wrapped up in himself, seeing only his own self-righteous deeds, catalogues his virtues before God, despising the poor publican who stands afar off. He exalts himself, gives himself over to self-praise, is self-centered, and goes away unjustified, condemned, and rejected by God.

The publican sees no good in himself, is overwhelmed with self-depreciation, far removed from anything which would take any credit for any good in himself, does not presume to lift his eyes to heaven, but with downcast countenance smites himself on his breast, and cries out, "God be merciful to me, a sinner."

Our Lord with great preciseness gives us the sequel of the story of these two men, one utterly devoid of humility, the other utterly submerged in the spirit of self-depreciation and lowliness of mind.

> I tell you, this man went down to his house justified rather than the other; for every one that exalteth himself shall be abased; and he that humbleth himself shall be exalted (Luke 18:14).

God puts a great price on humility of heart. It is good to be clothed with humility as with a garment. It is written, "God resisteth the proud, but giveth grace to the humble." That which brings the praying soul near to God is humility of heart. That which gives wings to prayer is lowliness of mind. That which gives ready access to the throne of grace is self-depreciation. Pride, self-esteem, and self-praise effectually shut the door of prayer. He who would come to God must approach Him with self hid from his eyes. He must not be puffed-up with self-conceit, nor be possessed with an over-estimate of his virtues and good works.

Humility is a rare Christian grace, of great price in the courts of heaven, entering into and being an inseparable condition of effectual praying. It gives access to God when other qualities fail. It takes many descriptions to describe it and many definitions to define it. It is a rare and retiring grace. Its full portrait is found only in the Lord Jesus Christ. Our prayers must be set low before they can ever rise high. Our prayers must have much of the dust on them before they can ever have much of the glory of the skies in them. In our Lord's teaching, humility has such prominence in His system of religion, and is such a distinguishing feature of His character, that to leave it out of His lesson on prayer would be very unseemly, would not comport with His character, and would not fit into His religious system.

The parable of the Pharisee and publican stands out in such bold relief that we must again refer to it. The Pharisee seemed to be inured to prayer. Certainly he should have known by that time how to pray, but alas, like many others, he seemed never to have learned this invaluable lesson. He leaves business and business hours and walks with steady and fixed steps up to the house of prayer. The position and place are well chosen by him. There is the sacred place, the sacred hour, and the sacred name, each and all invoked by this seemingly praying man. But this praying ecclesiastic, though schooled to prayer by training and by habit, prays not. Words are uttered by him, but words are not prayer. God hears his words only to condemn him. A death chill has come from those formal lips of prayer—a death curse from God is on his words of prayer. A solution of pride has entirely poisoned the prayer offering of that hour. His entire praying has been impregnated with self-praise, self-congratulation, and self-exaltation. That season of temple going has had no worship whatever in it.

On the other hand, the publican, smitten with a deep sense of his sins and his inward sinfulness, realizing how poor in spirit he is, how utterly devoid of anything like righteousness, goodness, or any quality which would commend him to God, his pride within utterly blasted and dead, falls down with humiliation and despair before God, while he utters a sharp cry for mercy for his sins and his guilt. A sense of sin and a realization of utter unworthiness has fixed the roots of humility deep down in his soul, and has oppressed self and eye and heart downward to the dust. This is the picture of humility against pride in praying. Here we see by sharp contrast the utter worthlessness of self-righteousness, self-exaltation, and self-praise in praying, and the great value, the beauty, and the divine commendation which comes to humility of heart, self-depreciation, and self-condemnation when a soul comes before God in prayer.

Happy are they who have no righteousness of their own to plead and no goodness of their own of which to boast. Humility flourishes in the soil of a true and deep sense of our sinfulness and our nothingness. Nowhere does humility grow so rankly and so rapidly and shine so brilliantly as when it feels all guilt, confesses all sin, and trusts all grace. "I the chief of sinners am, but Jesus died for me." That is praying ground, the ground of humility, low down, far away seemingly, but in reality brought nigh by the blood of the Lord Jesus Christ. God dwells in the lowly places. He makes such lowly places really the high places to the praying soul.

> Let the world their virtue boast,
>   Their works of righteousness;
> I, a wretch undone and lost,
>   Am freely saved by grace;
> Other title I disclaim,
>   This, only this, is all my plea,
> I the chief of sinners am,
>   But Jesus died for me.

Humility is an indispensable requisite of true prayer. It must be an attribute, a characteristic of prayer. Humility must be in the praying character as light is in the sun. Prayer has no beginning, no ending, no being, without humility. As a ship is made for the sea, so prayer is made for humility, and so humility is made for prayer.

Humility is not abstraction from self, nor does it ignore thought about self. It is a many-phased principle. Humility is born by looking at God and His holiness, and then looking at self and man's unholiness. Humility loves obscurity and silence, dreads applause, esteems the virtues of others, excuses their faults with mildness, easily pardons injuries, fears contempt less and less, and sees baseness and falsehood in pride. A true nobleness and greatness are in humility. It knows and reveres the inestimable riches of the cross, and the humiliations of Jesus Christ. It fears the luster of those virtues admired by men and loves those that are more sacred and which are prized by God. It draws comfort even from its own defects, through the abasement which they occasion. It prefers any degree of compunction before all light in the world.

Somewhat after this order of description is that definable grace of humility, so perfectly drawn in the publican's prayer, and so entirely absent from the prayer of the Pharisee. It takes many sittings to make a good picture of it.

Humility holds in its keeping the very life of prayer. Neither pride nor vanity can pray. Humility, though, is much more than the absence of vanity and pride. It is a positive quality, a substantial force, which energizes prayer. There is no power in prayer to ascend without it. Humility springs from a lowly estimate of ourselves and of our deservings. The Pharisee prayed not, though well schooled and habituated to pray, because there was no humility in his praying. The publican prayed, though banned by the public and receiving no encouragement from church sentiment, because he prayed in humility. To be clothed with humility is to be clothed with a praying garment. Humility is just feeling little because we *are* little. Humility is realizing our unworthiness because we *are* unworthy, the feeling and declaring ourselves sinners because we *are* sinners. Kneeling well becomes us as the attitude of prayer because it betokens humility.

The Pharisee's proud estimate of himself and his supreme contempt for his neighbor closed the gates of prayer to him, while humility opened wide those gates to the defamed and reviled publican.

That fearful saying of our Lord about the works of big, religious workers in the latter part of the Sermon on the Mount, is called out by proud estimates of work and wrong estimates of prayer:

> Many will say to me in that day, Lord, Lord, have we not prophesied in thy name? and in thy name have cast out devils? and in thy name done many wonderful works? And then will I profess unto them, I never knew you: depart from me, ye that work iniquity (Matt. 7:22, 23).

Humility is the first and last attribute of Christly religion, and the first and last attribute of Christly praying. There is no Christ without humility. There is no praying without humility. If thou wouldst learn well the art of praying, then learn well the lesson of humility.

How graceful and imperative does the attitude of humility become to us! Humility is one of the unchanging and exacting attitudes of prayer. Dust, ashes, earth upon the head, sackcloth for the body, and fasting for the appetites, were the symbols of humility for the Old Testament saints. Sackcloth, fasting, and ashes brought Daniel a lowliness before God and brought Gabriel to him. The angels are fond of the sackcloth-and-ashes men.

How lowly the attitude of Abraham, the friend of God, when pleading for God to stay His wrath against Sodom! "Which am but sackcloth and ashes." With what humility does Solomon appear before God! His grandeur is abased and his glory and majesty are retired as he assumes the rightful attitude before God: "I am but a little child, and know not how to go out or to come in."

The pride of doing sends its poison all through our praying. The same pride of being infects all our prayers, no matter how well-worded they may be. It was this lack of humility, this self-applauding, this self-exaltation, which kept the most religious man of Christ's day from being accepted of God. And the same thing will keep us in this day from being accepted of Him.

> O that now I might decrease!
> O that all I am might cease!
> Let me into nothing fall!
> Let my Lord be all in all.

4
Prayer and Devotion

Once as I rode out into the woods for my
health, in 1737, having alighted from my horse in a
retired place, as my manner commonly had been to
walk for divine contemplation and prayer, I had a
view that for me was extraordinary, of the glory of
the Son of God. As near as I can judge, this
continued about an hour; and kept me the greater
part of the time in a flood of tears and weeping
aloud. I felt an ardency of soul to be what I know
not otherwise how to express, emptied and
annihilated; to love Him with a holy and pure love;
to serve and follow Him; to be perfectly sanctified
and made pure with a divine and heavenly purity. —
Jonathan Edwards

Devotion has a religious signification. The root
of devotion is to devote to a sacred use. So that devotion
in its true sense has to do with religious worship. It
stands intimately connected with true prayer. Devotion
is the particular frame of mind found in one entirely
devoted to God. It is the spirit of reverence, of awe, of
godly fear. It is a state of heart which appears before
God in prayer and worship. It is foreign to everything

like lightness of spirit and is opposed to levity and noise and bluster. Devotion dwells in the realm of quietness and is still before God. It is serious, thoughtful, meditative.

Devotion belongs to the inner life and lives in the closet, but also appears in the public services of the sanctuary. It is a part of the very spirit of true worship, and is of the nature of the spirit of prayer.

Devotion belongs to the devout man whose thoughts and feelings are devoted to God. Such a man has a mind given up wholly to religion, and possesses a strong affection for God and an ardent love for His house. Cornelius was "a devout man, and one that feared God with all his house, which gave much alms to the people, and prayed to God alway" (Acts 10:2). "Devout men carried Stephen to his burial." "One Ananias, a devout man, according to the law," was sent unto Saul when he was blind, to tell him what the Lord would have him do. God can wonderfully use such men, for devout men are His chosen agents in carrying forward His plans.

Prayer promotes the spirit of devotion, while devotion is favorable to the best praying. Devotion furthers prayer and helps to drive prayer home to the object which it seeks. Prayer thrives in the atmosphere of true devotion. It is easy to pray when in the spirit of devotion. The attitude of mind and the state of heart implied in devotion make prayer effectual in reaching the throne of grace. God dwells where the spirit of devotion resides. All the graces of the Spirit are nourished and grow well in the environment created by devotion. Indeed, these graces grow nowhere else but here. The absence of a devotional spirit means death to the graces born in a renewed heart. True worship finds congeniality in the atmosphere made by a spirit of devotion. While prayer is helpful to devotion, at the same time devotion reacts on prayer and helps us to pray.

Devotion engages the heart in prayer. It is not an easy task for the lips to try to pray while the heart is absent from it. The charge which God at one time made against His ancient Israel was that they honored Him with their lips while their hearts were far from Him.

The very essence of prayer is the spirit of devotion. Without devotion prayer is an empty form, a vain round of words. Sad to say, much of this kind of prayer prevails today in the church. This is a busy age, bustling and active, and this bustling spirit has invaded the church of God. Its religious performances are many. The church works at religion with the order, precision, and force of real machinery. But too often it works with the heart-lessness of the machine. There is much of the treadmill movement in our ceaseless round and routine of religious doings. We pray without praying. We sing without singing with the Spirit and the understanding. We have music without the praise of God being in it or near it. We go to church by habit and come home all too gladly when the benediction is pronounced. We read our accustomed chapter in the Bible, and feel quite relieved when the task is done. We say our prayers by rote, as a schoolboy recites his lesson, and are not sorry when the Amen is uttered.

Religion has to do with everything but our hearts. It engages our hands and feet, it takes hold of our voices, it lays its hands on our money, it affects even the postures of our bodies, but it does not take hold of our affections, our desires, our zeal, and make us serious, desperately in earnest, and cause us to be quiet and worshipful in the presence of God. Social affinities attract us to the house of God, not the spirit of the occasion. Church membership keeps us after a fashion decent in outward conduct and with some shadow of loyalty to our baptismal vows, but the heart is not in the thing. It

remains cold, formal, and unimpressed amid all this outward performance, while we give ourselves over to self-
congratulation that we are doing wonderfully well
religiously.

Why all these sad defects in our piety? Why this
modern perversion of the true nature of the religion of
Jesus Christ? Why is the modern type of religion so
much like a jewel case with the precious jewels gone?
Why so much of this handling religion with the hands,
often not too clean or unsoiled, and so little of it felt in
the heart and witnessed in the life?

The great lack of modern religion is the spirit of
devotion. We hear sermons in the same spirit with which
we listen to a lecture or hear a speech. We visit the
house of God just as if it were a common place, on a
level with the theater, the lecture room, or the forum.
We look upon the minister of God not as the divinely-
called man of God, but merely as a sort of public speaker,
on a plane with the politician, the lawyer, or the average
speech maker, or lecturer. Oh, how the spirit of true and
genuine devotion would radically change all this for the
better! We handle sacred things just as if they were the
things of the world. Even the sacrament of the Lord's
Supper becomes a mere religious performance — no preparation for it beforehand, and no meditation and prayer
afterward. Even the sacrament of Baptism has lost much
of its solemnity and degenerated into a mere form, with
nothing specially in it.

We need the spirit of devotion, not only to salt our
secularities, but to make praying real prayers. We need
to put the spirit of devotion into Monday's business as
well as in Sunday's worship. We need the spirit of devotion, to recollect always the presence of God, to be
always doing the will of God, to direct all things always
to the glory of God.

The spirit of devotion puts God in all things. It puts God not merely in our praying and church going, but in all the concerns of life. "Whether therefore ye eat, or drink, or whatsoever ye do, do all to the glory of God" (I Cor. 10:31). The spirit of devotion makes the common things of earth sacred, and the little things great. With this spirit of devotion, we go to business on Monday directed by the very same influence, and inspired by the same influences by which we went to church on Sunday. The spirit of devotion makes a Sabbath out of Saturday and transforms the shop and the office into a temple of God.

The spirit of devotion removes religion from being a thin veneer and puts it into the very life and being of our souls. With it religion ceases to be doing a mere work and becomes a heart, sending its rich blood through every artery and beating with the pulsations of vigorous and radiant life.

The spirit of devotion is not merely the aroma of religion, but the stalk and stem on which religion grows. It is the salt which penetrates and makes savory all religious acts. It is the sugar which sweetens duty, self-denial, and sacrifice. It is the bright coloring which relieves the dullness of religious performances. It dispels frivolity and drives away all skin-deep forms of worship and makes worship a serious and deep-seated service, impregnating body, soul, and spirit with its heavenly infusion. Let us ask in all seriousness, has this highest angel of heaven, this heavenly spirit of devotion, this brightest and best angel of earth, left us? When the angel of devotion has gone, the angel of prayer has lost its wings, and it becomes a deformed and loveless thing.

The ardor of devotion is in prayer. In the fourth chapter of Revelation, verse eight, we read: "... and they rest not day and night, saying, Holy, holy, holy, Lord God

Almighty, which was, and is, and is to come." The inspiration and center of their rapturous devotion is the holiness of God. That holiness of God claims their attention, inflames their devotion. There is nothing cold, nothing dull, nothing wearisome about them or their heavenly worship. "They rest not day and night." What zeal! What unfainting ardor and ceaseless rapture! The ministry of prayer, if it be anything worthy of the name, is a ministry of ardor, a ministry of unwearied and intense longing after God and after His holiness.

The spirit of devotion pervades the saints in heaven and characterizes the worship of heaven's angelic intelligences. No devotionless creatures are in that heavenly world. God is there, and His very presence begets the spirit of reverence, of awe, and of filial fear. If we would be partakers with them after death, we must first learn the spirit of devotion on earth before we get there.

These living creatures in their restless, tireless, attitude after God, and their rapt devotion to His holiness, are the perfect symbols and illustrations of true prayer and its ardor. Prayer must be aflame. Its ardor must consume. Prayer without fervor is as a sun without light or heat, or as a flower without beauty or fragrance. A soul devoted to God is a fervent soul, and prayer is the creature of that flame. He only can truly pray who is all aglow for holiness, for God, and for heaven.

Activity is not strength. Work is not zeal. Moving about is not devotion. Activity often is the unrecognized symptom of spiritual weakness. It may be hurtful to piety when made the substitute for real devotion in worship. The colt is much more active than its mother, but she is the wheelhorse of the team, pulling the load without noise or bluster or show. The child is more active than the father, who may be bearing the rule and burdens of an empire on his heart and shoulders. Enthusiasm is more active than faith, though it cannot remove mountains nor call into action any of the omnipotent forces which faith can command.

A feeble, lively, showy religious activity may spring from many causes. There is much running around, much stirring about, much going here and there, in present-day church life, but sad to say, the spirit of genuine, heartfelt devotion is strangely lacking. If there be real spiritual life, a deep-toned activity will spring from it. But it is an activity springing from strength and not from weakness. It is an activity which has deep roots, many and strong.

In the nature of things, religion must show much of its growth above ground. Much will be seen and be evident to the eye. The flower and fruit of a holy life, abounding in good works, must be seen. It cannot be otherwise. But the surface growth must be based on a vigorous growth of unseen life and hidden roots. Deep down in the renewed nature must the roots of religion go which is seen on the outside. The external must have a deep internal groundwork. There must be much of the invisible and the underground growth, or else the life will be feeble and short-lived, and the external growth sickly and fruitless.

In the Book of the prophet Isaiah these words are written:

> But they that wait upon the Lord shall renew their strength; they shall mount up with wings as eagles; they shall run and not be weary; and they shall walk and not faint (40:31).

This is the genesis of the whole matter of activity and strength of the most energetic, exhaustless, and untiring nature. All this is the result of waiting on God.

There may be much of activity induced by drill, created by enthusiasm, the product of the weakness of the flesh, the inspiration of volatile, short-lived forces. Activity is often at the expense of more solid, useful elements, and generally to the total neglect of prayer. To be too busy with God's work to commune with God, to be busy with doing church work without taking time to talk to God about His work, is the highway to backsliding, and many people have walked therein to the hurt of their immortal souls.

Notwithstanding great activity, great enthusiasm, and much hurrah for the work, the work and the activity will be but blindness without the cultivation and the maturity of the graces of prayer.

5
Prayer, Praise and Thanksgiving

Dr. A. J. Gordon describes the impression made upon his mind by intercourse with Joseph Rabinowitz, whom Dr. Delitzsch considered the most remarkable Jewish convert since Saul of Tarsus: "We shall not soon forget the radiance that would come into his face as he expounded the Messianic psalms at our morning or evening worship, and how, as here and there he caught a glimpse of the suffering or glorified Christ, he would suddenly lift his hands and his eyes to heaven in a burst of adoration, exclaiming with Thomas after he had seen the nail-prints, 'My Lord, and my God.'"—D. M. McIntyre

Prayer, praise and thanksgiving all go in company. A close relationship exists between them. Praise and thanksgiving are so near alike that it is not easy to distinguish between them or define them separately. The Scriptures join these three things together. Many are the causes for thanksgiving and praise. The Psalms are filled with many songs of praise and hymns of thanksgiving, all pointing back to the results of prayer. Thanksgiving includes gratitude. In fact thanksgiving is but the expression of an inward conscious gratitude to God for mercies received. Gratitude is an inward emotion of the soul, involuntarily arising therein, while thanksgiving is the voluntary expression of gratitude.

Thanksgiving is oral, positive, active. It is the giving out of something to God. Thanksgiving comes out into the open. Gratitude is secret, silent, negative, passive, not showing its being till expressed in praise and thanksgiving. Gratitude is felt in the heart. Thanksgiving is the expression of that inward feeling.

Thanksgiving is just what the word itself signifies— the giving of thanks to God. It is giving something to God in words which we feel at heart for blessings received. Gratitude arises from a contemplation of the goodness of God. It is bred by serious meditation on what God has done for us. Both gratitude and thanksgiving point to and have to do with God and His mercies. The heart is consciously grateful to God. The soul gives expression to that heartfelt gratitude to God in words or acts.

Gratitude is born of meditation on God's grace and mercy. "The Lord hath done great things for us, whereof we are glad." Herein we see the value of serious meditation. "My meditation of him shall be sweet." Praise is begotten by gratitude and a conscious obligation to God for mercies given. As we think of mercies past, the heart is inwardly moved to gratitude.

> I love to think on mercies past,
>   And future good implore;
> And all my cares and sorrows cast
>   On Him whom I adore.

Love is the child of gratitude. Love grows as gratitude is felt, and then breaks out into praise and thanksgiving to God: "I love the Lord because he hath heard my voice and my supplication." Answered prayers cause gratitude, and gratitude brings forth a love that declares it will not cease praying: "Because he hath inclined his ear unto me, therefore will I call upon him as long as I live." Gratitude and love move to larger and increased praying.

Paul appeals to the Romans to dedicate themselves wholly to God, a living sacrifice, and the constraining motive is the mercies of God:

> I beseech you therefore, brethren, by the mercies of God, that ye present your bodies a living sacrifice, holy, acceptable unto God, which is your reasonable service (Rom. 12:1).

Consideration of God's mercies not only begets gratitude, but induces a large consecration to God of all we have and are. So that prayer, thanksgiving, and consecration are all linked together inseparably.

Gratitude and thanksgiving always looks back at the past though it may also take in the present. But prayer always looks to the future. Thanksgiving deals with things already received. Prayer deals with things desired, asked for, and expected. Prayer turns to gratitude and praise when the things asked for have been granted by God.

As prayer brings things to us which beget gratitude and thanksgiving, so praise and gratitude promote prayer and induce more praying and better praying.

Gratitude and thanksgiving forever stand opposed to all murmurings at God's dealings with us and all complainings at our lot. Gratitude and murmuring never abide in the same heart at the same time. An unappreciative spirit has no standing beside gratitude and praise. And true prayer corrects complaining and promotes gratitude and thanksgiving. Dissatisfaction at one's lot, and a disposition to be discontented with things which come to us in the providence of God, are foes to gratitude and enemies to thanksgiving.

The murmurers are ungrateful people. Appreciative men and women have neither the time nor disposition to stop and complain. The bane of the wilderness-journey of the Israelites on their way to Canaan was their proneness to murmur and complain against God and Moses. For this, God was several times greatly grieved, and it took the strong praying of Moses to avert God's wrath because of these murmurings. The absence of gratitude left no room nor disposition for praise and thanksgiving, just as it is so always. But when these same Israelites were brought through the Red Sea dry shod, while their enemies were destroyed, there was a song of praise led by Miriam, the sister of Moses. One of the leading sins of these Israelites was forgetfulness of God and His mercies, and ingratitude of soul. This brought forth murmurings and lack of praise, as it always does.

When Paul wrote to the Colossians to let the word of Christ dwell in their hearts richly and to let the peace of God rule therein, he said to them, "and be ye thankful," and added ". . . admonishing one another in psalms and hymns and spiritual songs, singing with grace in your hears to the Lord" (Col. 3:16).

Further on, in writing to these same Christians, he joins prayer and thanksgiving together: "Continue in prayer, and watch in the same with thanksgiving" (Col. 4:2).

And writing to the Thessalonians, he again joins them in union: "Rejoice evermore. Pray without ceasing. In everything give thanks: for this is the will of God in Christ Jesus concerning you" (I Thess. 5:16-18).

We thank Thee, Lord of heaven and earth,
Who hast preserved us from our birth;
Redeemed us oft from death and dread,
And with Thy gifts our table spread.

Wherever there is true prayer, there thanksgiving and gratitude stand hard by, ready to respond to the answer when it comes. For as prayer brings the answer, so the answer brings forth gratitude and praise. As prayer sets God to work, so answered prayer sets thanksgiving to work. Thanksgiving follows answered prayer just as day succeeds night.

True prayer and gratitude lead to full consecration, and consecration leads to more praying and better praying. A consecrated life is both a prayer life and a thanksgiving life.

The spirit of praise was once the boast of the primitive church. This spirit abode on the tabernacles of these early Christians as a cloud of glory out of which God shined and spoke. It filled their temples with the perfume of costly, flaming incense. That this spirit of praise is sadly deficient in our present-day congregations must be evident to evey careful observer. That it is a mighty force in projecting the gospel and its body of vital forces must be equally evident. To restore the spirit of praise to our congregations should be one of the main points with every true pastor. The normal state of the church is set forth in the declaration made to God in Psalm 65:1: "Praise waiteth for thee, O God, in Sion: and unto thee shall the vow be performed."

Praise is so distinctly and definitely wedded to prayer, so inseparably joined, that they cannot be divorced. Praise is dependent on prayer for its full volume and its sweetest melody.

Singing is one method of praise, not the highest it is

true, but it is the ordinary and usual form. The singing service in our churches has much to do with praise, for according to the character of the singing will be the genuineness or the measure of praise. The singing may be so directed as to have in it elements which deprave and debauch prayer. It may be so directed as to drive away everything like thanksgiving and praise. Much of modern singing in our churches is entirely foreign to anything like hearty, sincere praise to God.

The spirit of prayer and of true praise go hand in hand. Both are often entirely dissipated by the flippant, thoughtless, light singing in our congregations. Much of the singing lacks serious thought and is devoid of everything like a devotional spirit. Its lustiness and sparkle may not only dissipate all the essential features of worship, but may substitute the flesh for the spirit.

Giving thanks is the very life of prayer. It is its fragrance and music, its poetry and its crown. Prayer bringing the desired answer breaks out into praise and thanksgiving. So that whatever interferes with and injures the spirit of prayer necessarily hurts and dissipates the spirit of praise.

The heart must have in it the grace of prayer to sing the praise of God. Spiritual singing is not to be done by musical taste or talent, but by the grace of God in the heart. Nothing helps praise so mightily as a gracious revival of true religion in the church. The conscious presence of God inspires song. The angels and the glorified ones in heaven do not need artistic precentors to lead them, nor do they care for paid choirs to chime in with their heavenly doxologies of praise and worship. They are not dependent on singing schools to teach them the notes and scale of singing. Their singing involuntarily breaks forth from the heart.

God is immediately present in the heavenly assemblies of the angels and the spirits of just men made perfect. His glorious presence creates the song, teaches the singing, and impregnates their notes of praise. It is so on earth. God's presence begets singing and thanksgiving, while the absence of God from our congregations is the death of song, or, which amounts to the same, makes the singing lifeless, cold and formal. His conscious presence in our churches would bring back the days of praise and would restore the full chorus of song.

Where grace abounds, song abounds. When God is in the heart, heaven is present and melody is there, and the lips overflow out of the abundance of the heart. This is as true in the private life of the believer as it is so in the congregations of the saints. The decay of singing, the dying down and out of the spirit of praise in song, means the decline of grace in the heart and the absence of God's presence from the people.

The main design of all singing is for God's ear and to attract His attention and to please Him. It is "to the Lord," for His glory and to His honor. Certainly it is not for the glorification of the paid choir, to exalt the wonderful musical powers of the singers, nor is it to draw the people to the church, but it is for the glory of God and the good of the souls of the congregation. Alas! How far has the singing of choirs of churches of modern times departed from this idea! It is no surprise that there is no life, no power, no unction, no spirit, in much of the church singing heard in this day. It is sacrilege for any but sanctified hearts and holy lips to direct the singing part of the service of God's house of prayer. Much of the singing in churches would do credit to the opera house and might satisfy as mere entertainments, pleasing the ear, but as a part of real worship, having in it the spirit of praise and prayer, it is a fraud, an imposition on spiritually-minded people, and entirely unacceptable to God. The cry should go out afresh, "Let all the people praise the Lord," for "it is good to sing praises unto our God; for it is pleasant; and praise is comely."

The music of praise, for there is real music of soul in praise, is too hopeful and happy to be denied. All these are in the "giving of thanks." In Philippians, prayer is called "requests." "Let your requests be made known unto God," which describes prayer as an asking for a gift, giving prominence to the thing asked for, making it emphatic, something to be given by God and received by us, and not something to be done by us. And all this is closely connected with gratitude to God, "with thanksgiving, let your requests be made known unto God."

God does much for us in answer to prayer, but we need from Him many gifts, and for them we are to make special prayer. According to our special needs, so must our praying be. We are to be special and particular and bring to the knowledge of God by prayer, supplication, and thanksgiving our particular requests, the things we need, the things we greatly desire. And with it all, accompanying all these requests, there must be thanksgiving.

It is indeed a pleasing thought that what we are called upon to do on earth, to praise and give thanks, the angels in heaven and the redeemed disembodied spirits of the saints are doing also. It is still further pleasing to contemplate the glorious hope that what God wants us to do on earth we will be engaged in doing throughout an unending eternity. Praise and thanksgiving will be our blessed employment while we remain in heaven. Nor will we ever grow weary of this pleasing task.

Joseph Addison sets before us in verse this pleasing prospect:

Through every period of my life
   Thy goodness I'll pursue;
And after death, in distant worlds,
   The pleasing theme renew.

Through all eternity to Thee
   A grateful song I'll raise;
But Oh! eternity's too short
   To utter all Thy praise.

Excerpt from
Purpose in Prayer

Purpose in Prayer

6
Purpose in Prayer

The more praying there is in the world the better the world will be, the mightier the forces against evil everywhere. Prayer, in one phase of its operation, is a disinfectant and a preventive. It purifies the air; it destroys the contagion of evil. Prayer is no fitful, short-lived thing. It is no voice crying unheard and unheeded in the silence. It is a voice which goes into God's ear, and it lives as long as God's ear is open to holy pleas, as long as God's heart is alive to holy things.

God shapes the world by prayer. Prayers are deathless. The lips that uttered them may be closed in death, the heart that felt them may have ceased to beat, but the prayers live before God, and God's heart is set on them and prayers outlive the lives of those who uttered them; outlive a generation, outlive an age, outlive a world.

That man is the most immortal who has done the most and the best praying. They are God's heroes, God's saints, God's servants, God's vicegerents. A man can pray better because of the prayers of the past; a man can live holier because of the prayers of the past. The man of many and acceptable prayers has done the truest and greatest service to the incoming generation. The prayers of God's saints strengthen the unborn generation against

the desolating waves of sin and evil. Woe to the generation of sons who find their censers empty of the rich
incense of prayer; whose fathers have been too busy or
too unbelieving to pray, and perils inexpressible and con-
sequences untold are their unhappy heritage. Fortunate
are they whose fathers and mothers have left them a
wealthy patrimony of prayer.

The prayers of God's saints are the capital stock in
heaven by which Christ carries on His great work upon
earth. The great throes and mighty convulsions on earth
are the results of these prayers. Earth is changed, revo-
lutionized; angels move on more powerful, more rapid
wing, and God's policy is shaped as the prayers are more
numerous, more efficient.

It is true that the mightiest successes that come to
God's cause are created and carried on by prayer. God's
day of power; the angelic days of activity and power are
when God's church comes into its mightiest inheritance
of mightiest faith and mightiest prayer. God's conquering
days are when the saints have given themselves to mightiest prayer. When God's house on earth is a house of
prayer, then God's house in heaven is busy and all potent
in its plans and movements, then His earthly armies are
clothed with the triumphs and spoils of victory and His
enemies defeated on every hand.

God conditions the very life and prosperity of His
cause on prayer. The condition was put in the very existence of God's cause in this world. *Ask of Me* is the
one condition God puts in the very advance and triumph
of His cause.

Men are to pray—to pray for the advance of God's
cause. Prayer puts God in full force in the world. To a
prayerful man God is present in realized force; to a
prayerful church God is present in glorious power, and
the Second Psalm is the divine description of the estab-

lishment of God's cause through Jesus Christ. All inferior dispensations have merged in the enthronement of Jesus Christ. God declares the enthronement of His Son. The nations are incensed with bitter hatred against His cause. God is described as laughing at their enfeebled hate. The Lord will laugh; the Lord will have them in derision. "Yet have I set my king upon my holy hill of Zion." The decree has passed immutable and eternal:

> I will declare the decree: the Lord hath said unto me, Thou art my Son; this day have I begotten thee. Ask of me, and I shall give thee the heathen for thine inheritance, and the uttermost parts of the earth for thy possession. Thou shalt break them with a rod of iron; thou shalt dash them in pieces like a potter's vessel (Ps. 2:7-9).

Ask of Me is the condition—a praying people willing and obedient. "And men shall pray for him continually." Under this universal and simple promise men and women of old laid themselves out for God. They prayed and God answered their prayers, and the cause of God was kept alive in the world by the flame of their praying.

Prayer became a settled and only condition to move His Son's kingdom. "Ask, and it shall be given you; seek, and ye shall find; knock, and it shall be opened unto you" (Matt. 7:7). The strongest one in Christ's kingdom is he who is the best knocker. The secret of success in Christ's kingdom is the ability to pray. The one who can wield the power of prayer is the strong one, the holy one in Christ's kingdom. The most important lesson we can learn is how to pray.

Prayer is the keynote of the most sanctified life, of the holiest ministry. He does the most for God who is the highest skilled in prayer. Jesus Christ exercised His ministry after this order.

That we ought to give ourselves to God with regard to things both temporal and spiritual, and seek our satisfaction only in the fulfilling His will, whether He lead us by suffering, or by consolation, for all would be equal to a soul truly resigned. Prayer is nothing else but a sense of God's presence.—Brother Lawrence

Be sure you look to your secret duty; keep that up whatever you do. The soul cannot prosper in the neglect of it. Apostasy generally begins at the closet door. Be much in secret fellowship with God. It is secret trading that enriches the Christian.

Pray alone. Let prayer be the key of the morning and the bolt at night. The best way to fight against sin is to fight it on our knees. — Philip Henry

The prayer of faith is the only power in the universe to which the Great Jehovah yields. Prayer is the sovereign remedy.—Robert Hall

An hour of solitude passed in sincere and earnest prayer, or the conflict with and conquest over a single passion or subtle bosom sin will teach us more of thought, will more effectually awaken the faculty and form the habit of reflection than a year's study in the schools without them.—Samuel Taylor Coleridge

A man may pray night and day and deceive himself, but no man can be assured of his sincerity who does not pray. Prayer is faith passing into act. A union of the will and intellect realising in an intellectual act. It is the whole man that prays. Less than this is wishing or lip work, a sham or a mummery.

If God should restore me again to health I have determined to study nothing but the Bible. Literature is inimical to spirituality if it be not kept under with a firm hand.—Richard Cecil

Our sanctification does not depend upon
changing our works, but in doing that for God's
sake which we commonly do for our own. The time
of business does not with me differ from the time
of prayer. Prayer is nothing else but a sense of the
presence of God. — Brother Lawrence

Let me burn out for God. After all, whatever
God may appoint, prayer is the great thing. Oh that
I may be a man of prayer. — Henry Martyn

T he possibilities and necessity of prayer, its
power and results, are manifested in arresting and changing the purposes of God and in relieving the stroke of
His power. Abimelech was smitten by God:

So Abraham prayed unto God: and God healed Abimelech, and his wife, and his maidservants; and they bare
children. For the Lord had fast closed up all the wombs
of the house of Abimelech, because of Sarah Abraham's
wife (Gen. 20:17, 18).

Job's miserable mistaken comforters had so deported
themselves in their controversy with Job that God's wrath
was kindled against them. "My servant Job shall pray for
you," said God, "for him will I accept."

"And the Lord turned the captivity of Job when he
prayed for his friends."

Jonah was in dire condition when "the Lord sent out
a great wind into the sea, and there was a mighty tem-
pest." When lots were cast, "the lot fell upon Jonah."
He was cast overboard into the sea, but "the Lord had
prepared a great fish to swallow up Jonah. . . . Then
Jonah prayed unto the Lord his God out of the fish's

belly . . . and the Lord spake unto the fish, and it vomited out Jonah upon the dry land."

When the disobedient prophet lifted up his voice in prayer, God heard and sent deliverance.

Pharaoh was a firm believer in the possibilities of prayer and its ability to relieve. When staggering under the woeful curses of God, he pleaded with Moses to intercede for him. "Intreat the Lord for me," was his pathetic appeal four times repeated when the plagues were scourging Egypt. Four times were these urgent appeals made to Moses, and four times did prayer lift the dread curse from the hard king and his doomed land.

The blasphemy and idolatry of Israel in making the golden calf and declaring their devotions to it were a fearful crime. The anger of God waxed hot, and He declared that He would destroy the offending people. The Lord was very wroth with Aaron also, and to Moses He said, "Let Me alone that I may destroy them." But Moses prayed, and kept on praying; day and night he prayed forty days. He makes the record of his prayer struggle. "And I fell down," he says, "before the Lord, as at the first, forty days and nights: I did neither eat bread, nor drink water, because of all your sins which ye sinned, in doing wickedly in the sight of the Lord, to provoke him to anger. For I was afraid of the anger and hot displeasure, wherewith the Lord was wroth against you to destroy you. But the Lord hearkened unto me at that time also. And the Lord was very angry with Aaron to have destroyed him: and I prayed for Aaron also at the same time" (Deut. 9:18-20).

"Yet forty days, and Nineveh shall be overthrown." It was the purpose of God to destroy that great and wicked city. But Nineveh prayed, covered with sackcloth; sitting in ashes she cried "mightily to God," and "God repented of the evil, that he had said that he would do unto them; and he did it not" (Jonah 3:10).

The message of God to Hezekiah was: "Set thine house in order; for thou shalt die, and not live." Hezekiah turned his face toward the wall, and prayed unto the Lord, and said: "I beseech thee, O Lord, remember now how I have walked before thee in truth and with a perfect heart, and have done that which is good in thy sight." And Hezekiah wept. God told Isaiah to say to Hezekiah, "I have heard thy prayer, I have seen thy tears: behold, I will . . . add unto thy days fifteen years" (II Kings 20:1-6).

These men knew how to pray and how to prevail in prayer. Their faith in prayer was no passing attitude that changed with the wind or with their own feelings and circumstances. It was a fact that God heard and answered, that His ear was ever open to the cry of His children, and that the power to do what was asked of Him was commensurate with His willingness. And thus these men, strong in faith and in prayer, "subdued kingdoms, wrought righteousness, obtained promises, stopped the mouths of lions, Quenched the violence of fire, escaped the edge of the sword, out of weakness were made strong, waxed valiant in fight, turned to flight the armies of the aliens" (Heb. 11:33, 34).

Everything then, as now, was possible to the men and women who knew how to pray. Prayer, indeed, opened a limitless storehouse, and God's hand withheld nothing. Prayer introduced those who practiced it into a world of privilege and brought the strength and wealth of heaven down to the aid of finite man. What rich and wonderful power was theirs who had learned the secret of victorious approach to God! With Moses it saved a nation; with Ezra it saved a church.

And yet, strange as it seems when we contemplate the wonders of which God's people had been witness, there came a slackness in prayer. The mighty hold upon God that had so often struck awe and terror into the hearts of their enemies lost its grip. The people, back-slidden and apostate, had gone off from their praying — if the bulk of them had ever truly prayed. The Pharisee's cold and lifeless praying was substituted for any genuine approach to God, and because of that formal method of praying the whole worship became a parody of its real purpose. A glorious dispensation, and gloriously executed, was it by Moses, by Ezra, by Daniel and Elijah, by Hannah and Samuel; but the circle seems limited and shortlived; the praying ones were few and far between. They had no survivors, none to imitate their devotion to God, none to preserve the roll of the elect.

In vain had the decree established the divine order, the divine call. *Ask of Me*. From the earnest and fruitful crying to God they turned their faces to pagan gods and cried in vain for the answers that could never come. And so they sank into that godless and pitiful state that has lost its object in life when the link with the eternal has been broken. Their favored dispensation of prayer was forgotten; they knew not how to pray.

What a contrast to the achievements that brighten up other pages of holy writ. The power working through Elijah and Elisha in answer to prayer reached down even to the very grave. In each case a child was raised from the dead, and the powers of famine were broken. "The supplications of a righteous man avail much." Elijah was a man of like passions with us. He prayed fervently that it might not rain, and it rained not on the earth for three years and six months. And he prayed again, and the heaven gave rain, and the earth brought forth her fruit. Jonah prayed while imprisoned in the great fish, and he came to dry land, saved from storm and sea and monsters of the deep by the mighty energy of his praying.

How wide the gracious provision of the grace of praying as administered in that marvelous dispensation. They prayed wondrously. Why could not their praying save the dispensation from decay and death? Was it not because they lost the fire without which all praying degenerates into a lifeless form? It takes effort and toil and care to prepare the incense. Prayer is no laggard's work. When all the rich, spiced graces from the body of prayer have by labor and beating been blended and refined and intermixed, the fire is needed to unloose the incense and make its fragrance rise to the throne of God. The fire that consumes creates the spirit and life of the incense. Without fire prayer has no spirit; it is, like dead spices, for corruption and worms.

The casual, intermittent prayer is never bathed in this divine fire. For the man who thus prays is lacking in the earnestness that lays hold of God, determined not to let Him go until the blessing comes. "Pray without ceasing," counseled the great apostle. That is the habit that drives prayer right into the mortar that holds the building stones together. "You can do more than pray after you have prayed," said the godly Dr. A. J. Gordon, "but you cannot do more than pray until you have prayed." The story of every great Christian achievement is the history of answered prayer.

"The greatest and the best talent that God gives to any man or woman in this world is the talent of prayer," writes Principal Alexander Whyte. "And the best usury that any man or woman brings back to God when He comes to reckon with them at the end of this world is a life of prayer. And those servants best put their Lord's money 'to the exchangers' who rise early and sit late, as long as they are in this world, ever finding out and ever following after better and better methods of prayer, and ever forming more secret, more steadfast, and more spiritually fruitful habits of prayer, till they literally 'pray without ceasing,' and till they continually strike out into new enterprises in prayer, and new achievements, and new enrichments."

Martin Luther, when once asked what his plans for the following day were, answered: "Work, work, from early until late. In fact, I have so much to do that I shall spend the first three hours in prayer." Cromwell, too, believed in being much upon his knees. Looking on one occasion at the statues of famous men, he turned to a friend and said: "Make mine kneeling, for thus I came to glory."

It is only when the whole heart is gripped with the passion of prayer that the life-giving fire descends, for none but the earnest man gets access to the ear of God.

When thou feelest thyself most indisposed to prayer yield not to it, but strive and endeavour to pray even when thou thinkest thou canst not pray.—Arthur Hildersham

It was among the Parthians the custom that none was to give their children any meat in the morning before they saw the sweat on their faces, and you shall find this to be God's usual course not to give His children the taste of His delights till they begin to sweat in seeking after them.— Richard Baxter

Of all the duties enjoined by Christianity none is more essential and yet more neglected than prayer. Most people consider the exercise a fatiguing ceremony, which they are justified in abridging as much as possible. Even those whose profession or fears lead them to pray, pray with such languor and wanderings of mind that their

prayers, far from drawing down blessings, only
increase their condemnation.—François Fénelon

More praying and better is the secret of the
whole matter. More time for prayer, more relish and
preparation to meet God, to commune with God through
Christ—this has in it the whole of the matter. Our manner and matter of praying ill become us. The attitude
and relationship of God and the Son are the eternal relationship of Father and Son, of asking and giving—the
Son always asking, the Father always giving:

> Ask of me, and I shall give thee the heathen for thine
> inheritance, and the uttermost parts of the earth for thy
> possession. Thou shalt break them with a rod of iron;
> thou shalt dash them in pieces like a potter's vessel"
> (Ps. 2:8, 9).

Jesus is to be always praying through His people.
"And men shall pray for him continually." "For my house
shall be called a house of prayer for my peoples." We
must prepare ourselves to pray; to be like Christ, to pray
like Christ.

Man's access in prayer to God opens everything and
makes his impoverishment his wealth. All things are his
through prayer. The wealth and the glory—all things are
Christ's. As the light grows brighter and prophets take
in the nature of the restoration, the divine record seems
to be enlarged. "Thus saith the Lord, the Holy One of
Israel, and his Maker, Ask me of things to come concerning my sons, and concerning the work of my hands
command ye me. I have made the earth, and created man
upon it: I, even my hands, have stretched out the heavens,
and all their host have I commanded" (Isa. 45:11, 12).

To man is given to command God with all this authority and power in the demands of God's earthly kingdom. Heaven, with all it has, is under tribute to carry out the ultimate, final, and glorious purposes of God. Why then is the time so long in carrying out these wise benedictions for man? Why then does sin so long reign? Why are the oath-bound covenant promises so long in coming to their gracious end? Sin reigns, Satan reigns, sighing marks the lives of many; all tears are fresh and full.

Why is all this so? We have not prayed to bring the evil to an end; we have not prayed as we must pray. We have not met the conditions of prayer.

Ask of Me. Ask of God. We have not rested on prayer. We have not made prayer the sole condition. There has been violation of the primary condition of prayer. We have not prayed aright. We have not prayed at all. God is willing to give, but we are slow to ask. The Son, through His saints, is ever praying and God the Father is ever answering.

Ask of Me. In the invitation is conveyed the assurance of answer; the shout of victory is there and may be heard by the listening ear. The Father holds the authority and power in His hands. How easy is the condition, and yet how long are we in fulfilling the conditions! Nations are in bondage; the uttermost parts of the earth are still unpossessed. The earth groans; the world is still in bondage; Satan and evil hold sway.

The Father holds Himself in the attitude of giver, *Ask of Me*, and that petition to God the Father empowers all agencies, inspires all movements. The gospel is divinely inspired. Back of all its inspirations is prayer. *Ask of Me* lies back of all movements. Standing as the endowment of the enthroned Christ is the oath-bound covenant of the Father, "*Ask of Me*, and I will give thee the heathen for thine inheritance, and the uttermost parts of the earth for thy possession." "And men shall pray to him continually."

Ever are the prayers of holy men streaming up to God as fragrant as the richest incense. And God in many ways is speaking to us, declaring His wealth and our impoverishment. "I am the Maker of all things; the wealth and glory are mine. *Command ye me*."

We can do all things by God's aid, and can have the whole of His aid by asking. The gospel, in its success and power, depends on our ability to pray. The dispensations of God depend on man's ability to pray. We can have all that God has. *Command ye Me*. This is no figment of the imagination, no idle dream, no vain fancy. The life of the church is the highest life. Its office is to pray. Its prayer life is the highest life, the most odorous, the most conspicuous.

The Book of Revelation says nothing about prayer as a great duty, a hallowed service, but much about prayer in its aggregated force and energies. It is the prayer force ever living and ever praying; it is all saints' prayers going out as a mighty, living energy while the lips that uttered the words are stilled and sealed in death, while the living church has an energy of faith to inherit the forces of all the past praying and make it deathless.

The statement by the Baptist philosopher, John Foster, contains the purest philosophy and the simple truth of God, for God has no force and demands no conditions but prayer. "More and better praying will bring the surest and readiest triumph to God's cause; feeble, formal, listless praying brings decay and death. The church has its sheet-anchor in the closet; its magazine stores are there."

"I am convinced," Foster continues, "that every man who amidst his serious projects is apprized of his dependence upon God as completely as that dependence is a fact, will be impelled to pray and anxious to induce his serious friends to pray almost every hour. He will not without it promise himself any noble success any more than a mariner would expect to reach a distant coast by having his sails spread in a stagnation of air.

"I have intimated my fear that it is visionary to expect an unusual success in the human administration of religion unless there are unusual omens: now a most emphatical spirit of prayer would be such an omen; and the individual who should determine to try its last possible efficacy might probably find himself becoming a much more prevailing agent in his little sphere. And if the whole, or the greater number of the disciples of Christianity were with an earnest and unalterable resolution of each to combine that heaven should not withhold one single influence which the very utmost effort of conspiring and persevering supplication would obtain, it would be a sign that a revolution of the world was at hand."

Edward Payson, one of God's own, says of this statement of Foster, "Very few missionaries since the apostles, probably have tried the experiment. He who shall make the first trial will, I believe, effect wonders. Nothing that I could write, nothing that an angel could write, would be necessary to him who should make this trial.

"One of the principal results of the little experience which I have had as a Christian minister is a conviction that religion consists very much in giving God that place in our views and feelings which He actually fills in the universe. We know that in the universe He is all in all. So far as He is constantly all in all to us, so far as we comply with the Psalmist's charge to his soul, 'My soul, wait thou *only* upon God;' so far, I apprehend, have we advanced towards perfection. It is comparatively easy to wait upon God; but to wait upon Him *only* — to feel, so far as our strength, happiness, and usefulness are con-

cerned, as if all creatures and second causes were annihilated, and we were alone in the universe with God, is,
I suspect, a difficult and rare attainment. At least, I am
sure it is one which I am very far from having made. In
proportion as we make this attainment we shall find
everything easy; for we shall become, emphatically, men
of prayer; and we may say of prayer as Solomon says of
money, that it answereth all things."

This same John Foster said, when approaching death:
"I never prayed more earnestly nor probably with such
faithful frequency. 'Pray without ceasing' has been the
sentence repeating itself in the silent thought, and I am
sure it must be my practice till the last conscious hour
of life. Oh, why not throughout that long, indolent, inanimate half-century past?"

And yet this is the way in which we all act about
prayer. Conscious as we are of its importance, of its vital
importance, we yet let the hours pass away as a blank
and can only lament in death the irremediable loss.

When we calmly reflect upon the fact that the progress of our Lord's kingdom is dependent upon prayer, it
is sad to think that we give so little time to the holy
exercise. Everything depends upon prayer, and yet we
neglect it not only to our own spiritual hurt but also to
the delay and injury of our Lord's cause upon earth. The
forces of good and evil are contending for the world. If
we would, we could add to the conquering power of the
army of righteousness, and yet our lips are sealed, our
hands hang listlessly by our side, and we jeopardize the
very cause in which we profess to be deeply interested
by holding back from the prayer chamber.

Prayer is the one prime, eternal condition by which
the Father is pledged to put the Son in possession of the
world. Christ prays through His people. Had there been
importunate, universal, and continuous prayer by God's

people, long ere this the earth had been possessed for Christ. The delay is not to be accounted for by the inveterate obstacles, but by the lack of the right asking. We do more of everything else than of praying. As poor as our giving is, our contributions of money exceed our offerings of prayer. Perhaps in the average congregation fifty aid in paying, where one saintly, ardent soul shuts itself up with God and wrestles for the deliverance of the heathen world. Official praying on set or state occasions counts for nothing in this estimate. We emphasize other things more than we do the necessity of prayer.

We are saying prayers after an orderly way, but we have not the world in the grasp of our faith. We are not praying after the order that moves God and brings all divine influences to help us. The world needs more true praying to save it from the reign and ruin of Satan.

We do not pray as Elijah prayed. John Foster puts the whole matter to a practical point. "When the Church of God," he says, "is aroused to its obligation and duties and right faith to claim what Christ has promised — 'all things whatsoever' — a revolution will take place."

But not all praying is praying. The driving power, the conquering force in God's cause, is God Himself. "Call upon Me and I will answer thee and show thee great and mighty things which thou knowest not," is God's challenge to prayer. Prayer puts God in full force into God's work. "Ask me of things to come concerning my sons, and concerning the work of my hands command ye me" (Isa. 45:11) — God's *carte blanche* to prayer. Faith is only omnipotent when on its knees, and its outstretched hands take hold of God — then it draws to the utmost of God's capacity; for only a praying faith can get God's "all things whatsoever." Wonderful lessons are the Syrophoenician woman, the importunate widow, and the friend at midnight, of what dauntless prayer can do in mastering or defying conditions, in changing defeat into victory and triumphing in the regions of despair. Oneness with Christ, the acme of spiritual attainment, is glorious in all things; most glorious in that we can then "ask what we will and it shall be done unto us." Prayer in Jesus' name puts the crowning crown on God, because it glorifies Him through the Son and pledges the Son to give to men "whatsoever and anything" they shall ask.

In the New Testament the marvelous prayer of the Old Testament is put to the front that it may provoke and stimulate our praying, and it is preceded with a declaration, the dynamic energy of which we can scarcely translate. "The effectual fervent prayer of a righteous man availeth much. Elias [Elijah] was a man subject to like passions as we are, and he prayed earnestly that it might not rain: and it rained not on the earth by the space of three years and six months. And he prayed again, and the heaven gave rain, and the earth brought forth her fruit" (James 5:16b-18).

Our paucity in results, the cause of all leanness, is solved by the apostle James — ". . . ye have not, because ye ask not. Ye ask, and receive not, because ye ask amiss, that ye may spend it upon your lusts" (James 4:2b, 3).

That is the whole truth in a nutshell.

The potency of prayer hath subdued the strength of fire; it hath bridled the rage of lions, hushed anarchy to rest, extinguished wars, appeased the elements, expelled demons, burst the chains of death, expanded the gates of heaven, assuaged diseases, repelled frauds, rescued cities from destruction, stayed the sun in its course, and arrested the progress of the thunderbolt. Prayer is an all-efficient panoply, a treasure undiminished, a

mine which is never exhausted, a sky unobscured
by clouds, a heaven unruffled by the storm. It is the
root, the fountain, the mother of a thousand
blessings.—John Chrysostom

The prayers of holy men appease God's wrath,
drive away temptations, resist and overcome the
devil, procure the ministry and service of angels,
rescind the decrees of God. Prayer cures sickness
and obtains pardon; it arrests the sun in its course
and stays the wheels of the chariot of the moon; it
rules over all gods and opens and shuts the
storehouses of rain, it unlocks the cabinet of the
womb and quenches the violence of fire; it stops
the mouths of lions and reconciles our suffering
and weak faculties with the violence of torment
and violence of persecution; it pleases God and
supplies all our need.—Jeremy Taylor

More things are wrought by prayer
Than this world dreams of. Wherefore, let thy voice
Rise like a fountain for me night and day.
For what are men better than sheep or goats,
That nourish a blind life within the brain,
If, knowing God, they lift not hands of prayer
Both for themselves and those who call them friend?
For so the whole round earth is every way
Bound by gold chains about the feet of God.
                                        —Alfred Tennyson

Perfect prayer is only another name for love.
—François Fénelon

Excerpts from

Power Through Prayer

Much Time Should Be Given to Prayer
Prayer Marks Spiritual Leadership
Preachers Need the Prayers of the People

7
Much Time Should Be Given to Prayer

The great masters and teachers in Christian
doctrine have always found in prayer their highest
source of illumination. Not to go beyond the limits
of the English Church, it is recorded of Bishop
Andrews that he spent five hours daily on his
knees. The greatest practical resolves that have
enriched and beautified human life in Christian
times have been arrived at in prayer — Henry P.
Liddon

While many private prayers, in the nature of
things, must be short; while public prayers, as a rule,
ought to be short and condensed; while there is ample
room for and value put on ejaculatory prayer — yet in our
private communions with God time is a feature essential
to its value. Much time spent with God is the secret of
all successful praying. Prayer which is felt as a mighty
force is the mediate or immediate product of much time
spent with God. Our short prayers owe their point and
efficiency to the long ones that have preceded them. The

short prevailing prayer cannot be prayed by one who has not prevailed with God in a mightier struggle of long continuance. Jacob's victory of faith could not have been gained without that all-night wrestling. God's acquaintance is not made by pop calls. God does not bestow his gifts on the casual or hasty comers and goers. Much with God alone is the secret of knowing him and of influence with him. He yields to the persistency of a faith that knows him. He bestows his richest gifts upon those who declare their desire for and appreciation of those gifts by the constancy as well as earnestness of their importunity. Christ, who in this as well as other things is our example, spent many whole nights in prayer. His custom was to pray much. He had his habitual place to pray. Many long seasons of praying make up his history and character. Paul prayed day and night. It took time from very important interests for Daniel to pray three times a day. David's morning, noon, and night praying were doubtless on many occasions very protracted. While we have no specific account of the time these Bible saints spent in prayer, yet the indications are that they consumed much time in prayer, and on some occasions long seasons of praying was their custom.

We would not have any think that the value of their prayers is to be measured by the clock, but our purpose is to impress on our minds the necessity of being much alone with God; and that if this feature has not been produced by our faith, then our faith is of a feeble and surface type.

The men who have most fully illustrated Christ in their character, and have most powerfully affected the world for him, have been men who spent so much time with God as to make it a notable feature of their lives. Charles Simeon devoted the hours from four till eight in the morning to God. Mr. Wesley spent two hours daily in prayer. He began at four in the morning. Of him, one who knew him well wrote: "He thought prayer to be more his business than anything else, and I have seen him come out of his closet with a serenity of face next to shining." John Fletcher stained the walls of his room by the breath of his prayers. Sometimes he would pray all night; always, frequently, and with great earnestness. His whole life was a life of prayer. "I would not rise from my seat," he said, "without lifting my heart to God." His greeting to a friend was always: "Do I meet you praying?" Luther said: "If I fail to spend two hours in prayer each morning, the devil gets the victory through the day. I have so much business I cannot get on without spending three hours daily in prayer." He had a motto: "He that has prayed well has studied well."

Archbishop Leighton was so much alone with God that he seemed to be in a perpetual meditation. "Prayer and praise were his business and his pleasure," says his biographer. Bishop Ken was so much with God that his soul was said to be God-enamored. He was with God before the clock struck three every morning. Bishop Asbury said: "I propose to rise at four o'clock as often as I can and spend two hours in prayer and meditation." Samuel Rutherford, the fragrance of whose piety is still rich, rose at three in the morning to meet God in prayer. Joseph Alleine arose at four o'clock for his business of praying till eight. If he heard other tradesmen plying their business before he was up, he would exclaim: "O how this shames me! Doth not my Master deserve more than theirs?" He who has learned this trade well draws at will, on sight, and with acceptance of heaven's unfailing bank.

One of the holiest and among the most gifted of Scotch preachers says: "I ought to spend the best hours in communion with God. It is my noblest and most fruitful employment, and is not to be thrust into a corner. The morning hours, from six to eight, are the most uninterrupted and should be thus employed. After tea is my best hour, and that should be solemnly dedicated to God. I ought not to give up the good old habit of prayer before going to bed; but guard must be kept against sleep. When I awake in the night, I ought to rise and pray. A little time after breakfast might be given to intercession." This was the praying plan of Robert McCheyne. The memorable Methodist band in their praying shame us. "From four to five in the morning, private prayer; from five to six in the evening, private prayer."

John Welch, the holy and wonderful Scotch preacher, thought the day ill spent if he did not spend eight or ten hours in prayer. He kept a plaid that he might wrap himself when he arose to pray at night. His wife would complain when she found him lying on the ground weeping. He would reply: "O woman, I have the souls of three thousand to answer for, and I know not how it is with many of them!"

8

Prayer Marks
Spiritual Leadership

Give me one hundred preachers who fear
nothing but sin and desire nothing but God, and I
care not a straw whether they be clergymen or
laymen: such alone will shake the gates of hell and
set up the kingdom of heaven on earth. God does
nothing but in answer to prayer. — John Wesley

The apostles knew the necessity and worth of
prayer to their ministry. They knew that their high commission as apostles, instead of relieving them from the
necessity of prayer, committed them to it by a more
urgent need. For this reason they were exceedingly jealous else some other important work should exhaust their
time and prevent their praying as they ought. Thus, they
appointed laymen to look after the delicate and engross-
ing duties of ministering to the poor, that they (the apostles) might, unhindered, "give themselves continually to
prayer and to the ministry of the word." Prayer is put
first, and their relation to prayer is put most strongly —
"give themselves to it," making a business of it, surren-

dering themselves to praying, putting fervor, urgency, perseverance, and time in it.

How holy, apostolic men devoted themselves to this divine work of prayer! "Night and day praying exceedingly," says Paul. "We will give ourselves continually to prayer" is the consensus of apostolic devotement. How these New Testament preachers laid themselves out in prayer for God's people! How they put God in full force into their churches by their praying! These holy apostles did not vainly fancy that they had met their high and solemn duties by delivering faithfully God's word, but their preaching was made to stick and tell by the ardor and insistence of their praying. Apostolic praying was as taxing, toilsome, and imperative as apostolic preaching. They prayed mightily day and night to bring their people to the highest regions of faith and holiness. They prayed mightier still to hold them to this high spiritual altitude. The preacher who has never learned in the school of Christ the high and divine art of intercession for his people will never learn the art of preaching, though homiletics be poured into him by the ton, and though he be the most gifted genius in sermon making and sermon delivery.

The prayers of apostolic, saintly leaders do much in making saints of those who are not apostles. If the church leaders in after years had been as particular and fervent in praying for their people as the apostles were, the sad, dark times of worldliness and apostasy had not marred the history and eclipsed the glory and arrested the advance of the church. Apostolic praying makes apostolic saints and keeps apostolic times of purity and power in the church.

What loftiness of soul, what purity and elevation of motive, what unselfishness, what self-sacrifice, what exhaustive toil, what ardor of spirit, what divine tact are requisite to be an intercessor for men!

The preacher is to lay himself out in prayer for his people; not that they might be saved, simply, but that they be mightily saved. The apostles laid themselves out in prayer that their saints might be perfect; not that they should have a little relish for the things of God, but that they "might be filled with all the fullness of God." Paul did not rely on his apostolic preaching to secure this end, but "for this cause he bowed his knees to the Father of our Lord Jesus Christ." Paul's praying carried Paul's converts farther along the highway of sainthood than Paul's preaching did. Epaphras did as much or more by prayer for the Colossian saints than by his preaching. He labored fervently, always in prayer for them that "they might stand perfect and complete in all the will of God."

Preachers are preeminently God's leaders. They are primarily responsible for the condition of the church. They shape its character, give tone and direction to its life.

Much every way depends on these leaders. They shape the times and the institutions. The church is divine, the treasure it incases is heavenly, but it bears the imprint of the human. The treasure is in earthen vessels, and it smacks of the vessel. The church of God makes, or is made by, its leaders. Whether it makes them or is made by them, it will be what its leaders are; spiritual if they are so, secular if they are, conglomerate if its leaders are. Israel's kings gave character to Israel's piety. A church rarely revolts against or rises above the religion of its leaders. Strongly spiritual leaders; men of holy might, at the lead, are tokens of God's favor; disaster and weakness follow the wake of feeble or worldly leaders. Israel had fallen low when God gave children to be their princes and babes to rule over them. No happy state is predicted by the prophets when children oppress God's Israel and women rule over them. Times of spiritual leadership are times of great spiritual prosperity to the church.

Prayer is one of the eminent characteristics of strong spiritual leadership. Men of mighty prayer are men of might and mold things. Their power with God has the conquering tread.

How can a man preach who does not get his message fresh from God in the closet? How can he preach without having his faith quickened, his vision cleared, and his heart warmed by his closeting with God? Alas, for the pulpit lips which are untouched by this closet flame. Dry and unctionless they will ever be, and truths divine will never come with power from such lips. As far as the real interests of religion are concerned, a pulpit without a closet will always be a barren thing.

A preacher may preach in an official, entertaining, or learned way without prayer, but between this kind of preaching and sowing God's precious seed with holy hands and prayerful, weeping hearts there is an immeasurable distance.

A prayerless ministry is the undertaker for all God's truth and for God's church. He may have the most costly casket and the most beautiful flowers, but it is a funeral, notwithstanding the charmful array. A prayerless Christian will never learn God's truth; a prayerless ministry will never be able to teach God's truth. Ages of millennial glory have been lost by a prayerless church. The coming of our Lord has been postponed indefinitely by a prayerless church. Hell has enlarged herself and filled her dire caves in the presence of the dead service of a prayerless church.

The best, the greatest offering, is an offering of prayer. If the preachers of the twentieth century will learn well the lesson of prayer, and use fully the power of prayer, the millennium will come to its noon ere the century closes. "Pray without ceasing" is the trumpet call to the preachers of the twentieth century. If the twentieth century will get their texts, their thoughts, their words, their sermons in their closets, the next century will find a new heaven and a new earth. The old sin-stained and sin-eclipsed heaven and earth will pass away under the power of a praying ministry.

9

Preachers Need the Prayers of the People

If some Christians that have been complaining of their ministers had said and acted less before men and had applied themselves with all their might to cry to God for their ministers—had, as it were, risen and stormed heaven with their humble, fervent, and incessant prayers for them—they would have been much more in the way of success.—Jonathan Edwards

Somehow the practice of praying in particular for the preacher has fallen into disuse or become discounted. Occasionally have we heard the practice arraigned as a disparagement of the ministry, being a public declaration by those who do it of the inefficiency of the ministry. It offends the pride of learning and self-sufficiency, perhaps, and these ought to be offended and rebuked in a ministry that is so derelict as to allow them to exist.

Prayer, to the preacher, is not simply the duty of his profession, a privilege, but it is a necessity. Air is not more necessary to the lungs than prayer is to the preacher. It is absolutely necessary for the preacher to pray. It is an absolute necessity that the preacher be prayed for. These two propositions are wedded into a union which ought never to know any divorce: *the preacher must pray; the preacher must be prayed for.* It will take all the praying he can do, and all the praying he can get done, to meet the fearful responsibilities and gain the largest, truest success in his great work. The true preacher, next to the cultivation of the spirit and fact of prayer in himself, in their intensest form, covets with a great covetousness the prayers of God's people.

The holier a man is, the more does he estimate prayer; the clearer does he see that God gives himself to the praying ones, and that the measure of God's revelation to the soul is the measure of the soul's longing, importunate prayer for God. Salvation never finds its way to a prayerless heart. The Holy Spirit never abides in a prayerless spirit. Preaching never edifies a prayerless soul. Christ knows nothing of prayerless Christians. The gospel cannot be projected by a prayerless preacher. Gifts, talents, education, eloquence, God's call, cannot abate the demand of prayer, but only intensify the necessity for the preacher to pray and to be prayed for. The more the preacher's eyes are opened to the nature, responsibility, and difficulties in his work, the more will he see, and if he be a true preacher the more will he feel, the necessity of prayer; not only the increasing demand to pray himself, but to call on others to help him by their prayers.

Paul is an illustration of this. If any man could project the gospel by dint of personal force, by brain power, by culture, by personal grace, by Gods's apostolic commission, God's extraordinary call, that man was Paul. That the preacher must be a man given to prayer, Paul is an eminent example. That the true apostolic preacher must have the prayers of other good people to give to his ministry its full quota of success, Paul is a preeminent example. He asks, he covets, he pleads in an impassioned way for the help of all God's saints. He knew that in the spiritual realm, as elsewhere, in union there is strength; that the concentration and aggregation of faith, desire, and prayer increased the volume of spiritual force until it became overwhelming and irresistible in its power. Units of prayer combined, like drops of water, make an ocean which defies resistance. So Paul, with his clear and full apprehension of spiritual dynamics, determined to make his ministry as impressive, as eternal, as irresistible as the ocean, by gathering all the scattered units of prayer and precipitating them on his ministry. May not the solution of Paul's preeminence in labors and results, and impress on the church and the world, be found in this fact that he was able to center on himself and his ministry more of prayer than others? To his brethren at Rome he wrote: "Now I beseech you, brethren, for the Lord Jesus Christ's sake, and for the love of the Spirit, that ye strive together with me in your prayers to God for me" (15:30). To the Ephesians he says: "Praying always with all prayer and supplication in the Spirit, and watching thereunto with all perseverance and supplication for all saints; And for me, that utterance may be given unto me, that I may open my mouth boldly, to make known the mystery of the gospel" (6:18, 19). To the Colossians he emphasizes: "Withal praying also for us, that God would open unto us a door of utterance, to speak the mystery of Christ, for which I am also in bonds: That I may make it manifest as I ought to speak" (4:3, 4). To the Thessalonians he says sharply, strongly: "Brethren, pray for us" (I Thess. 5:25). Paul calls on the Corinthian church to help him: "Ye also helping together by prayer for us ..." (II Cor. 1:11). This was to be part of their work. They were to lay to the helping hand of prayer. He, in an additional and closing charge to the Thessalonian church about the importance and necessity of their prayers, says: "Finally, brethren, pray for us, that the word of the Lord may have free course, and be glorified, even as it is with you: And that we may be delivered from unreasonable and wicked men ..." (II Thess. 3:1, 2). He impresses the Philippians that all his trials and opposition can be made subservient to the spread of the gospel by the efficiency of their prayers for him. Philemon was to prepare a lodging for him, for through Philemon's prayer Paul was to be his guest.

Paul's attitude on this question illustrates his humility and his deep insight unto the spiritual forces which project the gospel. More than this, it teaches a lesson for all times, that if Paul was so dependent on the prayers of God's saints to give his ministry success, how much greater the necessity that the prayers of God's saints be centered on the ministry of today!

Paul did not feel that this urgent plea for prayer was to lower his dignity, lessen his influence, or depreciate his piety. What if it did? Let dignity go, let influence be destroyed, let his reputation be marred — he must have their prayers. Called, commissioned, chief of the apostles as he was, all his equipment was imperfect without the prayers of his people. He wrote letters everywhere, urging them to pray for him. Do you pray for your preacher? Do you pray for him in secret? Public prayers are of little worth unless they are founded on or followed up by private praying. The praying ones are to the preacher as Aaron and Hur were to Moses. They hold up his hands and decide the issue that is so fiercely raging around them.

The plea and purpose of the apostles were to put the

church to praying. They did not ignore the grace of cheerful giving. They were not ignorant of the place which religious activity and work occupied in the spiritual life; but not one nor all of these, in apostolic estimate or urgency, could at all compare in necessity and importance with prayer. The most sacred and urgent pleas were used, the most fervid exhortations, the most comprehensive and arousing words were uttered to enforce the all-important obligation and necessity of prayer.

"Put the saints everywhere to praying" is the burden of the apostolic effort and the keynote of apostolic success. Jesus Christ had striven to do this in the days of his personal ministry. As he was moved by infinite compassion at the ripened fields of earth perishing for lack of laborers—and pausing in his own praying—he tries to awaken the stupid sensibilities of his disciples to the duty of prayer as he charges them, "Pray ye therefore the Lord of the harvest, that he will send forth labourers into his harvest" (Matt. 9:38). "And he spake a parable unto them to this end, that men ought always to pray and not to faint" (Luke 18:1).

Prayer and Praying Men

10

Praying Saints of the Old Testament

The Holy Spirit will give to the praying saint
the brightness of an immortal hope, the music of a
deathless song, in His baptism and communion
with the heart, He will give sweeter and more
enlarged visions of heaven until the taste for other
things will pall, and other visions will grow dim
and distant. He will put notes of other worlds in
human hearts until all earth's music is discord and
songless.—Edward M. Bounds

Old Testament history is filled with accounts of praying saints. The leaders of Israel in those early days were noted for their praying habits. Prayer is the one thing which stands out prominently in their lives.

To begin with, note the incident in Joshua, tenth chapter, where the very heavenly bodies were made subject to prayer. A prolonged battle was on between the Israelites and their enemies, and when night was rapidly coming on, and it was discovered that a few more hours of daylight were needful to ensure victory for the Lord's hosts, Joshua, that sturdy man of God, stepped into the breach, with prayer. The sun was too rapidly declining in the west for God's people to reap the full fruits of a noted victory, and Joshua, seeing how much depended upon the occasion, cried out in the sight and in the hearing of Israel, "Sun, stand thou still upon Gibeon, and thou, Moon, in the valley of Ajalon" (Josh. 10:12b). And the sun actually stood still and the moon stopped on her course at the command of this praying man of God, till the Lord's people had avenged themselves upon the Lord's enemies.

Jacob was not a strict pattern of righteousness, prior to his all-night praying. Yet he was a man of prayer and believed in the God of prayer. So we find him swift to call upon God in prayer when he was in trouble. He was fleeing from home, fearing Esau, on his way to the home of Laban, a kinsman. As night came on, he lighted on a certain place to refresh himself with sleep, and as he slept he had a wonderful dream in which he saw the angels of God ascending and descending on a ladder which stretched from earth to heaven. It was no wonder when he awoke he was constrained to exclaim, "Surely the Lord is in this place; and I knew it not" (Gen. 28:16b).

Then it was he entered into a very definite covenant with almighty God, and in prayer vowed a vow unto the Lord, saying, "If God will be with me, and will keep me in this way that I go, and will give me bread to eat, and raiment to put on, So that I come again to my father's house in peace; and shall the Lord be my God: And this stone which I have set for a pillar shall be God's house: and of all that thou shalt give me I will surely give the tenth unto thee" (Gen. 28:20b-22).

With a deep sense of his utter dependence upon God, and desiring above all the help of God, Jacob conditioned his prayer for protection, blessing, and guidance by a solemn vow. Thus Jacob supported his prayer to God by a vow.

Twenty years had passed while Jacob tarried at the house of Laban, and he had married two of Laban's daughters, and God had given him children. He had increased largely in wealth, and he resolved to leave that place and return home to where he had been reared. Nearing home it occurred to him that he must meet his brother Esau, whose anger had not abated notwithstanding the passage of many years. God, however, had said to him, "Return to thy country, and to thy kindred, and I will deal well with thee" (Gen. 32:9b). In this dire emergency doubtless God's promise and his vow made long ago came to his mind, and he took himself to an all-night season of prayer. Here comes to our notice that strange, inexplicable incident of the angel struggling with Jacob all night long, till Jacob at last obtained the victory. "I will not let thee go except thou bless me" (Gen. 32:26b). And then and there, in answer to his earnest, pressing, and importunate praying, he was richly blessed personally and his name was changed. But even more than that, God went ahead of Jacob's desire and strangely moved upon the angry nature of Esau, and lo and behold, when Jacob met him next day, Esau's anger had abated, and he vied with Jacob in showing kindness to his brother who had wronged him. No explanation of this remarkable change in the heart of Esau is satisfactory which leaves out prayer.

Samuel, the mighty intercessor in Israel and a man of God, was the product of his mother's prayer. Hannah is a memorable example of the nature and benefits of importunate praying. No son had been born to her and she yearned for a man child. Her whole soul was in her desire. So she went to the house of worship, where Eli, the priest of God, was and, staggering under the weight of which bore down on her heart, she was beside herself and seemed to be really intoxicated. Her desires were too intense for articulation. She poured out her soul in prayer before the Lord (see I Sam. 1:15b). Insuperable natural difficulties were in the way, but she "multiplied her praying," as the passage means, till her God-lightened heart and her bright face recorded the answer to her prayers, and Samuel was hers by a conscious faith and a nation was restored by faith.

Samuel was born in answer to the vowful prayer of Hannah, for the solemn covenant which she made with God if He would grant her request must not be left out of the account in investigating this incident of a praying woman and the answer she received. It is suggestive in James 5:15 that "The prayer of faith shall save the sick." The word translated means a vow. So that prayer in its highest form of faith is that prayer which carries the whole man as a sacrificial offering. Thus devoting the whole man himself and his all to God in a definite, intelligent vow, never to be broken, in a quenchless and impassioned desire for heaven — such an attitude of self-devotement to God mightily helps praying. Samson is somewhat of a paradox when we examine his religious character. But amid all his faults, which were grave in the extreme, he knew the God who hears prayer, and he knew how to talk to God.

No farness to which Israel had gone, no depth to which Israel had fallen, no chains however iron with which Israel was bound but that their cry to God easily spanned the distance, fathomed the depths, and broke the chains. It was the lesson they were ever learning and always forgetting, that prayer always brought God to their deliverance, and that there was nothing too hard for God to do for His people. We find all of God's saints in straits at different times in some way or another. Their straits are, however, often the heralds of their great triumphs. But for whatever cause their straits come, or of what kind soever, there is no strait of any degree of direness or from any source whatsoever of any nature whatsoever, from which prayer could not extricate them. The great strength of Samson does not relieve him nor extricate him out of his straits. Read what the Scriptures say:

> And when he came unto Lehi, the Philistines shouted against him: and the Spirit of the Lord came mightily upon him, and the cords that were upon his arms became as flax that was burnt with fire, and his bands loosed from off his hands.
>
> And he found a new jawbone of an ass, and put forth his hand, and took it, and slew a thousand men therewith.
>
> And Samson said, With the jawbone of an ass, heaps upon heaps, with the jaw of an ass have I slain a thousand men.
>
> And it came to pass, when he had made an end of speaking, that he cast away the jawbone out of his hand, and called that place Ramath—lehi.
>
> And he was sore athirst, and called on the Lord, and said, Thou hast given this great deliverance into the hand of thy servant: and now shall I die for thirst, and fall into the hand of the uncircumcised?
>
> But God clave an hollow place that was in the jaw, and there came water thereout; and when he had drunk, his spirit came again, and he revived ... (Judg. 15:14-20).

We have another incident in the case of this strange Old Testament character, showing how, when in great straits, their minds involuntarily turned to God in prayer. However irregular in life they were, however far from God they departed, however sinful they might be when trouble came upon these men, they invariably called upon

God for deliverance, and, as a rule, when they repented God heard their cries and granted their requests. This incident comes at the close of Samson's life, and shows us how his life ended.

Read the record as found in Judges, sixteenth chapter. Samson had formed an alliance with Delilah, a heathen woman, and she, in connivance with the Philistines, sought to discover the source of his immense strength. Three successive times she failed, and at last by her persistence and womanly arts persuaded Samson to divulge to her the wonderful secret. So in an unsuspecting hour he disclosed to her the fact that the source of his strength was in his hair which had never been cut; and she deprived him of his great physical power by cutting off his hair. She called for the Philistines and they came and put out his eyes and otherwise mistreated him.

On an occasion when the Philistines were gathered together to offer a great sacrifice to Dagon, their idol god, they called for Samson to make sport for them. And the following is the account as he stood there presumably the laughingstock of these enemies of his and of God.

> And Samson said unto the lad that held him by the hand, Suffer me that I may feel the pillars whereupon the house standeth, that I may lean upon them.
>
> Now the house was full of men and women; and all the lords of the Philistines were there; and there were upon the roof about three thousand men and women, that beheld while Samson made sport.
>
> And Samson called unto the Lord and said, O Lord God, remember me, I pray thee, and strengthen me, I pray thee, only this once, O God, that I may be at once avenged of the Philistines for my two eyes. And Samson took hold of the two middle pillars upon which the house stood, and on which it was borne up, of the one with his right hand, and of the other with his left.

And Samson said, Let me die with the Philistines. And he bowed himself with all his might; and the house fell upon the lords, and upon all the people that were therein. So the dead which he slew at his death were more than they which he slew in his life (Judg. 16:26-30).

Bishop Lambeth and Wainwright had a great M. E. Mission in Osaka, Japan. One day the order came from high up that no more meetings would be allowed in the city by Protestants. Lambeth and Wainwright did all they could but the high officials were obstinate and unrelenting. They then retired to the room of prayer. Supper time came and the Japanese girl came to summon them to their meal, but she fell under the power of prayer. Mrs. Lambeth came to find what the matter was and fell under the same power. They then rose and went to the mission hall and opened it: and at once commenced meeting. God fell upon the assembly and two of the sons of the city officials came to the altar and were saved. Next morning one of the officials in authority came to the mission and said, "Go on with your meetings, you will not be interrupted." The Osaka daily paper came out with box car letters saying, "THE CHRISTIAN'S GOD CAME TO TOWN LAST NIGHT."—H. C. Morrison

Jonah, the man who prayed in the fish's belly, brings to view another remarkable instance of these Old Testament worthies who were given to prayer. This man Jonah, a prophet of the Lord, was a fugitive from God and from the place of duty. He had been sent on a mission of warning to wicked Nineveh, and had been commanded to cry out against them, "for their wickedness is come up before me," said God. But Jonah, through fear or otherwise, declined to obey God, and took passage on a ship for Tarshish, fleeing from God. He seems to have overlooked the plain fact that the same God who had sent him on that alarming mission had His eye upon him as he hid himself on board that vessel. A storm arose as the vessel was on its way to Tarshish, and it was decided to throw Jonah overboard in order to appease God and to avert the destruction of the boat and of all on board. But God was there as He had been with Jonah from the beginning. He had prepared a great fish to swallow Jonah, in order to arrest him, to defeat him in his flight from the post of duty, and to save Jonah that he might help to carry out the purposes of God.

It was Jonah who was in the fish's belly, in that great strait, and passing through a strange experience, who called upon God, who heard him and caused the fish to vomit him out on dry land. What possible force could rescue him from this fearful place? He seemed hopelessly lost, in "the belly of hell," as good as dead and damned. But he prays — what else can he do? And this is just what he had been accustomed to do when in trouble before.

> I cried by reason of mine affliction unto the Lord, and he heard me; out of the belly of hell cried I, and thou heardest my voice (Jonah 2:2).

> And the Lord spake unto the fish, and it vomited out Jonah upon the dry land (Jonah 2:10).

Like others he joined prayer to a vow he had made, for he says in his prayer, "But I will sacrifice unto thee with the voice of thanksgiving; I will pay that that I have vowed. Salvation is of the Lord" (Jonah 2:9).

Prayer was the mighty force which brought Jonah from "the belly of hell." Prayer, mighty prayer, has secured the end. Prayer brought God to the rescue of unfaithful Jonah, despite his sin of fleeing from duty, and God could not deny his prayer. Nothing is too hard for prayer because nothing is too hard for God.

That answered prayer of Jonah in the fish's belly in its mighty results became an Old Testament type of the miraculous power displayed in the resurrection of Jesus Christ from the dead. Our Lord puts His seal of truth upon the fact of Jonah's prayer and resurrection.

Nothing can be simpler than these cases of God's mighty deliverance. Nothing is plainer than that prayer has to do with God directly and simply. Nothing is clearer than that prayer has its only worth and significance in the great fact that God hears and answers prayer. This the Old Testament saints strongly believed. It is the one fact that stands out continuously and prominently in their lives. They were essentially men of prayer.

How greatly we need a school to teach the art of praying! This simplest of all arts and mightiest of all forces is ever in danger of being forgotten or depraved. The further we get away from our mother's knees, the further do we get away from the true art of praying. All our after schooling and our after teachers unteach us the lessons of prayer. Men prayed well in Old Testament times because they were simple men and lived in simple times. They were childlike, lived in childlike times, and had childlike faith.

In citing the Old Testament saints noted for their praying habits, by no means must David be overlooked, a man who preeminently was a man of prayer. With him prayer was a habit, for we hear him say, "Evening, and morning, and at noon, will I pray, and cry aloud." Prayer with the sweet psalmist of Israel was no strange occupation. He knew the way to God and was often found in that way. It is no wonder we hear his call so clear and impressive, "O come, let us worship and bow down; let us kneel before the Lord our maker." He knew God as the one being who could answer prayer: "O thou that hearest prayer, unto thee shall all flesh come."

When God smote the child born of Bathsheba, because David had by his grievous sins given occasion of the enemies of God to blaspheme, it is no surprise that we find him engaged in a week's praying, asking God for the life of the child. The habit of his life asserted itself in this great emergency in his home, and we find him fasting and praying for the child to recover. The fact that God denied his request does not at all affect the question of David's habit of praying. Even though he did not receive what he asked for, his faith in God was not in the least affected. The fact is that while God did not give him the life of that baby boy, He afterward gave him another son, even Solomon. So that possibly the latter son was a far greater blessing to him than would have been the child for whom he prayed.

In close connection with this season of prayer, we must not overlook David's penitential praying when Nathan, by command of God, uncovered David's two great sins of adultery and murder. At once David acknowledged his wickedness, saying unto Nathan, "I have sinned." And as showing his deep grief over his sin, his heartbroken spirit, and his genuine repentance, it is only necessary to read Psalm 51 where confession of sin, deep humiliation, and prayer are the chief ingredients of the Psalm.

David knew where to find a sin-pardoning God, and was received back again and had the joys of salvation restored to him by earnest, sincere, penitential praying. Thus are all sinners brought into the divine favor, thus do they find pardon, and thus do they find a new heart.

The entire Book of Psalms brings prayer to the front,

and prayer fairly bristles before our eyes as we read this devotional book of the Scriptures.

Nor must even Solomon be overlooked in the famous catalogue of men who prayed in Old Testament times. Whatever their faults, they did not forget the God who hears prayer nor did they cease to seek the God of prayer. While this wise man in his later life departed from God, and his sun set under a cloud, we find him praying at the commencement of his reign.

Solomon went to Gibeon to offer sacrifice, which always meant that prayer went in close companionship with sacrifice, and while there, the Lord appeared to Solomon in a vision by night, saying unto him, "Ask what I shall give thee." The sequel shows the material out of which Solomon's character was formed. What was his request?

> O Lord my God, thou hast made thy servant king instead of David my father: and I am but a little child: I know not how to go out or come in.
>
> And thy servant is in the midst of thy people which thou hast chosen, a great people, that cannot be numbered nor counted for multitude.
>
> Give therefore thy servant an understanding heart to judge thy people, that I may discern between good and bad: for who is able to judge this thy so great a people (I Kings 3:7-9)?

We do not wonder that it is recorded as a result of such praying:

> And the speech pleased the Lord, that Solomon had asked this thing.
>
> And God said unto him, Because thou hast asked this thing, and hast not asked for thyself long life; neither hast asked riches for thyself, nor hast asked the life of

thine enemies; but hast asked for thyself understanding
to discern judgment;

Behold, I have done according to thy words; lo, I have
given thee a wise and an understanding heart; so that
there was none like thee before thee, neither after thee
shall any arise like unto thee.

And I have also given thee that which thou hast not
asked, both riches, and honour; so that there shall not
be any among the kings like unto thee all thy days
(I Kings 3:10-12).

What praying was this! What self-deprecation and
simplicity! "I am but a little child." How he specified
the one thing needful! And see how much more he received than that for which he asked!

Take the remarkable prayer at the dedication of the
temple. Possibly this is the longest recorded prayer in
God's Word. How comprehensive, pointed, intensive, it
is! Solomon could not afford to lay the foundations of
God's house in anything else but in prayer. And God
heard this prayer as he heard him before, "Now when
Solomon had made an end of praying, the fire came down
from heaven, ... and the glory of the Lord filled the
house." Thus, God attested the acceptance of this house
of worship and of Solomon, the praying king.

The list of these Old Testament saints given to prayer
grows as we proceed and is too long to notice at length
all of them. But the name of Isaiah, the great evangelical
prophet, and that of Jeremiah, the weeping prophet, must
not be left out of the account. Still others might be
mentioned. These are sufficient, and with their names
we may close the list. Let careful readers of the Old
Scriptures keep the prayer question in mind, and they
will see how great a place prayer occupied in the minds
and lives of the men of those early days.

11

Moses, the Mighty Intercessor

Intercessory Prayer is a powerful means of grace to the praying man. Martyn observes that at times of inward dryness and depression, he had often found a delightful revival in the act of praying for others for their conversion, or sanctification, or prosperity in the work of the Lord. His dealings with God for them about these gifts and blessings were for himself the divinely natural channel of a renewed insight into his own part and lot in Christ, into Christ as his own rest and power, into the "perfect freedom" of an entire yielding of himself to his Master for His work.—H. C. G. Moule

Prayer unites with the purposes of God and lays itself out to secure those purposes. How often would the wise and benign will of God fail in its rich and beneficent ends by the sins of the people if prayer had not come in to arrest wrath and make the promise sure! Israel as a nation would have met their just destruction and their just fate after their apostasy with the golden calf had it not been for the interposition and unfainting importunity of Moses' forty days' and forty nights' praying!

Marvelous was the effect of the character of Moses by his marvelous praying. His near and sublime intercourse with God in the giving of the law worked no transfiguration of character like the tireless praying of those forty days in prayer with God. It was when he came down from that long struggle of prayer that his face shone with such dazzling brightness. Our mounts of transfiguration and the heavenly shining in character and conduct are born of seasons of wrestling prayer. All-night praying has changed many a Jacob, the supplanter, into Israel, a prince, who has power with God and with men.

No mission was more majestic in purpose and results than that of Moses, and none was more responsible, diligent, and difficult. In it we are taught the sublime ministry and rule of prayer. Not only is it the medium of supply and support, but it is a compassionate agency through which the pitying long-suffering of God has an outflow. Prayer is a medium to restrain God's wrath, that mercy might rejoice against judgment.

Moses himself and his mission were the creation of prayer. Thus it is recorded: "When Jacob was come into Egypt, and your fathers cried unto the Lord, then the Lord sent Moses and Aaron, which brought your fathers out of Egypt, and made them dwell in this place" (I Sam. 12:8). This is the genesis of the great movement for the deliverance of the Hebrews from Egyptian bondage.

The great movements of God have had their origin and energy in and were shaped by prayers of men. Prayer has directly to deal with God. Other ends, collateral and incidental, are secured by prayer, but mainly, almost solely, prayer has to deal with God. He is pleased to order His policy and base His action on the prayers of

His saints. Prayer influences God greatly. Moses cannot do God's great work, though God-commissioned, without praying much. Moses cannot govern God's people and carry out the divine plans without having his censer filled full of the incense of prayer. The work of God cannot be done without the fire and fragrance are always burning, ascending, and perfuming.

Moses' prayers are often found relieving the terrible stroke of God's wrath. Four times were the prayers of Moses solicited by Pharaoh to relieve him of the fearful stroke of God's wrath. "Intreat the Lord," most earnestly begged Pharaoh of Moses, while the loathsome frogs were upon him. "And Moses cried unto the Lord because of the frogs which he had brought against Pharaoh. And the Lord did according to the word of Moses . . ." (Exod. 8:12b, 13a). When the grievous plague of flies had corrupted the whole land, Pharoah again piteously cried out to Moses, "Intreat for me." Moses went out from Pharaoh and entreated the Lord, and the Lord again did according to the word of Moses. The mighty thunderings and hail in their alarming and destructive fury extorted from this wicked king the very same earnest appeal to Moses, "Intreat the Lord." And Moses went out from the city into privacy, and alone with almighty God he "spread abroad his hands unto the Lord: and the thunders and hail ceased, and the rain was not poured upon the earth" (Exod. 9:33b).

Though Moses was the man of law, yet with him prayer asserted its mighty force. With him, as in the more spiritual dispensation, it could have been said, "My house is the house of prayer."

Moses accepts at its full face value the foundation principle of praying that prayer has to do with God. With Abraham we saw this clearly and strongly enunciated. With Moses it is clearer and stronger still if possible. It declared that prayer affected God, that God was influenced in His conduct by prayer, and that God hears and answers prayer even when the hearing and answering might change His conduct and reverse His action. Stronger than all other laws, and more inflexible than any other decree, is the decree, "Call upon me and I will answer you."

Moses lived near God and had the freest and most unhindered and boldest access to God, but this, instead of abating the necessity of prayer, made it more necessary, obvious, and powerful. Familiarity and closeness to God gives relish, frequency, point, and potency to prayer. Those who know God the best are the richest and most powerful in prayer. Little acquaintance with God, and strangeness and coldness to Him, make prayer a rare and feeble thing.

There were conditions of extremity to which Moses was reduced which prayer did not relieve, but there is no position of extremity which baffles God when prayer puts God into the matter.

Moses' mission was a divine one. It was ordered, directed, and planned by God. The more there is of God in a movement, the more there is of prayer, conspicuous and controlling. Moses' prayer rule of the church illustrates the necessity of courage and persistence in prayer. For forty days and forty nights was Moses pressing his prayer for the salvation of the Lord's people. So intense was his concern for them which accompanied his long season of praying, that bodily infirmities and appetites were retired. How strangely the prayers of a righteous man affect God is evident from the exclamation of God to Moses, "Now therefore let me alone, that my wrath may wax hot against them, and that I may consume them: and I will make of thee a great nation" (Exod. 32:10). The presence of such an influence over God fills us with astonishment, awe, and fear. How lofty, bold, and devoted must be such a pleader!

Read this from the divine record:

> And Moses returned unto the Lord, and said, Oh, this people have sinned a great sin, and have made them gods of gold.
>
> Yet now, if thou wilt forgive their sin—; and if not, blot me, I pray thee, out of thy book which thou hast written.
>
> And the Lord said unto Moses, Whosoever hath sinned against me, him will I blot out of my book.
>
> Therefore now go, lead the people unto the place of which I have spoken unto thee: behold, mine Angel shall go before thee (Exod. 32:31-34).

The rebellion of Korah was the occasion of God's anger flaming out against the whole congregation of Israel, who sympathized with these rebels. Again Moses appears on the stage of action, this time having Aaron to join him in intercession for these sinners against God. But it only shows that in a serious time like this Moses knew to whom to go for relief and was encouraged to pray that God would stay His wrath and spare Israel. Here is what is said about the matter:

> And the Lord spake unto Moses and unto Aaron, saying,
>
> Separate yourselves from among this congregation, that I may consume them in a moment.
>
> And they fell on their faces, and said, O God, the God of the spirits of all flesh, shall one man sin, and wilt thou be wroth with all the congregation (Num. 16:20-22)?

The assumption, pride, and rebellion of Miriam, sister of Moses, in which she had the presence and sympathy of Aaron, put the praying and the spirit of Moses in the noblest and most amiable light. Because of her sin God smote her with leprosy. But Moses made tender and earnest intercession for his sister who had so grievously offended God, and his prayer saved her from the fearful and incurable malady.

The record is intensely interesting, and follows just here:

> And the anger of the Lord was kindled against them . . . and the cloud departed from off the tabernacle; and, behold, Miriam became leprous, white as snow: and Aaron looked upon Miriam, and, behold, she was leprous.
>
> And Aaron said unto Moses, Alas, my lord, I beseech thee, lay not the sin unto us, wherein we have done foolishly, and wherein we have sinned.
>
> Let her not be as one dead, of whom the flesh is half consumed when he cometh out of his mother's womb.
>
> And Moses cried unto the Lord, saying, Heal her now, O God, I beseech thee.
>
> And the Lord said unto Moses, If her father had but spit in her face, should she not be ashamed seven days? let her be shut out from the camp seven days, and after that let her be received in again (Num. 12:9-14).

The murmurings of the children of Israel furnished conditions which called into play the full forces of prayer. They impressively bring out the intercessory feature of prayer and disclose Moses in his great office as an intercessor before God in behalf of others. It was at Marah, where the waters were bitter and the people grievously murmured against Moses and God.

Here is the Scripture account:

> And when they came to Marah, they could not drink of the waters of Marah, for they were bitter: therefore the name of it was called Marah.

> And the people murmured against Moses, saying, What shall we drink?
>
> And He cried unto the Lord; and the Lord showed him a tree, which when he had cast into the waters, the waters were made sweet: there he made for them a statute and an ordinance, and there he proved them (Exod. 15:23-25).

How many of the bitter places of the earth have been sweetened by prayer the records of eternity alone will disclose.

Again at Taberah the people complained, and God became angry with them, and Moses came again to the front and stepped into the breach and prayed for them. Here is the brief account:

> And when the people complained, it displeased the Lord: and the Lord heard it; and his anger was kindled; and the fire of the Lord burnt among them, and consumed them that were in the uttermost parts of the camp.
>
> And the people cried unto Moses; and when Moses prayed unto the Lord, the fire was quenched (Num. 11:1, 2).

Moses got what he asked for. His praying was specific and God's answer was likewise specific. Always was he heard by almighty God when he prayed, and always was he answered by God. Once the answer was not specific. He had prayed to go into Canaan. The answer came but not what he asked for. He was given a vision of the Promised Land, but he was not allowed to go over Jordan into that land of promise. It was a prayer on the order of Paul's when he prayed three times for the removal of the thorn in the flesh. But the thorn was not removed. Grace, however, was vouchsafed which made the thorn a blessing.

It must not be thought that because the Ninetieth

Psalm is incorporated with what is known as the "Psalms of David" that David was the author of it. By general consent it is attributed to Moses, and it gives us a sample of the praying of this giver of the law of God to the people. It is a prayer worth studying. It is sacred to us because it has been the requiem uttered over our dead for years that are past and gone. It has blessed the grave of many a sleeping saint. But its very familiarity may cause us to lose its full meaning. Wise will we be if we digest it, not for the dead, but for the living, that it may teach us how to live, how to pray while living, and how to die. "So teach us to number our days, that we may apply our hearts unto wisdom . . . establish thou the work of our hands upon us; yea, the work of our hands establish thou it" (Ps. 90:12, 17b).

12
Paul, the Teacher of Prayer

Fletcher of Madeley, a great teacher of a century and a half ago, used to lecture to the young theological students. He was one of the fellow-workers with Wesley and a man of most saintly character. When he had lectured on one of the great topics of the Word of God, such as the Fullness of God's Holy Spirit or on the power and blessing that He meant His people to have, he would close the lecture and say, "That is the theory; now will those who want the practice come along up to my room?" And again and again they closed their books and went away to his room, where the hour's theory would be followed by one or two hours of prayer. — Hubert Brooke

How instant, strenuous, persistent, and pathetic was Paul's urgency of prayer upon those to whom he wrote and spoke! "I exhort therefore," says he, writing to Timothy, "that, first of all, supplications, prayers, intercessions, and giving of thanks, be made for all men" (I Tim. 2:1). This he meant was to be the prime deposit and truth for the church. First of all, before all things, to the front of all things, the church of Christ was to be a praying church, was to pray for men, was to pray for all men. He charged the Philippians to this effect: "Be careful for nothing; but in every thing, by prayer and supplication with thanksgiving, let your requests be made known unto God" (Phil. 4:6). The church must be anxious about nothing. In everything prayer must be made. Nothing was too small about which to pray. Nothing was too great for God to overcome.

Paul lays it down as a vital, all-essential injunction in writing to the church at Thessalonica, "Rejoice evermore. Pray without ceasing. In every thing give thanks: for this is the will of God in Christ Jesus concerning you" (I Thess. 5:16-18). The church must give itself to unceasing prayer. Never was prayer to cease in the church. This was the will of God concerning His church on earth.

Paul was not only given to prayer himself, but he continually and earnestly urged it in a way that showed its vital importance. He was not only insistent in urging prayer upon the church in his day, but he urged persistent praying. "Continue in prayer and watch in the same," was the keynote of all his exhortations on prayer. "Praying always with all prayer and supplication," was the way he pressed this important matter upon the people. "I will, therefore," I exhort, this is my desire, my mind upon this question, "that men pray everywhere, without wrath and doubting." As he prayed after this fashion himself, he could afford to press it upon those to whom he ministered.

Paul was a leader by appointment and by universal recognition and acceptance. He had many mighty forces in this ministry. His conversion, so conspicuous and radical, was a great force, a perfect magazine of aggressive and defensive warfare. His call to the apostleship was clear, luminous, and convincing. But these forces were not the divinest energies which brought forth the largest results to his ministry. Paul's course was more distinctly shaped and his career rendered more powerfully successful by prayer than by any other force.

It is no surprise then that he should give such prominence to prayer in his preaching and writing. We could not expect it to be otherwise. As prayer was the highest exercise in his personal life, so also prayer assumed the same high place in his teaching. His example of prayer added force to his teaching on prayer. His practice and his teaching ran in parallel lines. There was no inconsistency in the two things.

Paul was the chiefest of the apostles as he was chief in prayer. If he was the first of the apostles, prayer conspired to that end. Hence he was all the better qualified to be a teacher on prayer. His praying fitted him to teach others what prayer was and what prayer could do. And for this reason he was competent to urge upon the people that they must not neglect prayer. Too much depended upon it.

He was first in prayer for this cause. For the reason that on him centered more saintly praying than on anyone else, he became the first in apostleship. The crown of martyrdom was the highest crown in the royalty of heaven, but prayer put this crown of martyrdom on his head.

He who would teach the people to pray must first himself be given to prayer. He who urges prayer on others must first tread the path of prayer himself. And just in proportion as preachers pray, will they be disposed to urge prayer upon those to whom they preach. Moreover, just in proportion as preachers pray, will they be fitted to preach on prayer. If that course of reasoning be true, would it be legitimate to draw the conclusion that the reason why there is so little preaching on prayer in these modern times is because preachers are not praying men?

We might stake the whole question of the absolute necessity and the possibilities of prayer in this dispensation on Paul's attitude toward prayer. If personal force, if the energy of a strong will, if profound convictions, if personal culture and talents, and if the divine call and the divine empowerment — if any one of these, or all of them united, could direct the church of God without prayer, then logically prayer would be unnecessary. If profound piety and unswerving consecration to a high purpose, if impassioned loyalty to Jesus Christ, if any or all of these could exist without devoted prayer, or lift a church leader above the necessity of prayer, then Paul was above its use. But if the great and gifted, the favored and devoted Paul felt the necessity of unceasing prayer, and realized that it was urgent and pressing in regard to its claims and necessity, and if he felt that it was clamorous and insistent that the church should pray without ceasing, then he and his brethren in the apostolate should be aided by universal and mighty praying.

Paul's praying and his commands and the urgency with which he pressed upon the church to pray is the most convincing proof of the absolute necessity of prayer as a great moral force in the world, an indispensable and inalienable factor in the progress and spread of the gospel, and in the development of personal piety. In Paul's view, there was no church success without prayer, and no piety without prayer, in fact without much prayer. A church out of whose life streams prayer as the incense flames went out of the censer, and a leadership out of whose character, life, and habits flames prayer as imposing, conspicuous, and spontaneous as the fragrant incense flamed, this was the leadership for God.

To pray everywhere, to pray in everything, to continue

instant in prayer, and to pray without ceasing, thus Paul spoke as a commentator on the divine uses and the nature of prayer.

Timothy was very dear to Paul, and the attachment was mutual and intensified by all their affinities. Paul found in Timothy those elements which fitted him to be his spiritual successor, at least the depository and the leader of the great spiritual principles and forces which were essential to the establishment and prosperity of the church. These primary and vital truths he would enforce on and radicate in Timothy. Paul regarded Timothy as one to whom fundamental and vital truths might be committed, who would preserve them truly, and who would commit them inviolate to the future. So he gave to Timothy this deposit of prayer for all ages as found in I Timothy 2:1.

Let it be noted before we go any further that Paul wrote directly under the superintendency of the Holy Spirit, who guarded Paul against error and who suggested the truths which Paul taught. We hold definitely without compromise in the least to the plenary inspiration of the Scriptures, and as Paul's writings are part and parcel of those sacred writings, then Paul's Epistles are portions of the Scriptures or the Word of God. This being true, the doctrine of prayer which Paul affirmed is the doctrine of the Holy Spirit. His Epistles are of the Word of God, inspired, authentic, and of divine authority. So that prayer as taught by Paul is the doctrine which almighty God would have His church accept, believe, and practice.

These words to Timothy, therefore, were divinely inspired words. This section of Holy Writ is much more than merely suggestive, and is far more than a broad, bare outline on prayer. It is so instructive about prayer, about how men ought to pray, how businessmen should pray, and so forceful about the reasons why men ought to pray, that it needs to be strongly and insistently pressed.

Here are Paul's words to Timothy on prayer:

I exhort therefore, that, first of all, supplications, prayers, intercessions, and giving of thanks, be made for all men;

For kings, and for all that are in authority; that we may lead a quiet and peaceable life in all godliness and honesty.

For this is good and acceptable in the sight of God our Saviour;

Who will have all men to be saved, and to come unto the knowledge of the truth.

For there is one God, and one mediator between God and men, the man Christ Jesus;

Who gave himself a ransom for all, to be testified in due time.

I will therefore that men pray every where, lifting up holy hands, without wrath and doubting (I Tim. 2:1-6, 8).

In this prayer section we have set forth by Paul the inheritance and practice of every Christian in all ages. It is a *vade mecum* in the great business of praying. It gives us a view of the energy and many-sidedness of prayer. First in point of time in all excellence of all duties is prayer. It must be first in all occupations. So exacting and imperative in its import and power is prayer that it stands first among spiritual values. He that prays not is not at all. He is naught, less than naught. He is below zero, so far as Christ and God and heaven are concerned. Not simply among the first things does prayer stand on a level with other things, but first of the first, to the very forefront, does Paul put prayer with all his heart. "I exhort that first of all."

His teaching is that praying is the most important of all things on earth. All else must be restrained, retired, to give it primacy. Put it first, and keep its primacy. The conflict is about the primacy of prayer. Defeat and victory lie in this one thing. To make prayer secondary is to discrown it. It is to fetter and destroy prayer. If prayer is put first, then God is put first, and victory is assured. Prayer must either reign in the life or must abdicate. Which shall it be?

According to Paul, "supplications, prayers, intercessions and giving of thanks," all these elements of prayer and forms of prayer are to be offered for men. Prayer is offered for things, for all things, for all temporal good, and for all spiritual good and grace, but in these directions Paul rises to the highest results and purposes of prayer. Men are to be affected by prayer. Their good, their character, conduct, and destiny are all involved in prayer. In this regard prayer moves along the highest way and pursues its loftiest end. We are cognizant and consonant with things, with blessings and bestowments, with matters and things which touch men, but men themselves are here set forth as the objects of prayer. This broadens and ennobles prayer. Men, through the whole sweep and range of their conditions, are to be held in the mighty grasp of prayer.

Paul's teaching is to the effect that prayer is essentially a thing of the inner nature. The spirit within us prays. So note Paul's directions: "I will therefore that men pray every where ... without wrath." "Wrath" is a term which denotes the natural, internal motion of plants and fruits, swelling with juice. The natural juices are warmed into life, and rise by the warmth of spring. Man has in him natural juices which rise as does the sap. Warmth, heat, all stages of passions and desires, every degree of feeling, these spontaneously rise under provocation. Guard against and suppress them. Man cannot pray with these natural feelings rising in him, cultivated, cherished and continued there. Prayer is to be without these. "Without wrath." Higher, better, nobler inspiration are to lift prayer upward. "Wrath" depresses prayer, hinders it, suppresses it.

The word "without" means making no use of, having no association with, apart from, aloof from. The natural, unrenewed heart has no part in praying. Its heat and all its nature juices poison and destroy praying. The nature of prayer is deeper than nature. We cannot pray by nature, even by the kindliest and the best nature.

Prayer is the true test of character. Fidelity to our conditions and trueness to our relations are often evinced by our prayerfulness. Some conditions give birth to prayer. They are the soil which germinates and perfects prayer. To pray under some circumstances seems very fitting. Not to pray in some conditions seems heartless and discordant. The great storms of life, when we are helpless and without relief, or are devoid of assuagement, are the natural and providential conditions of prayer.

Widowhood is a great sorrow. It comes to saintly women as well as to others. True widows there are who are saintly. They are to be honored and their sorrow is divine. Their piety is aromatic and lightened by their bruised hearts. Here is Paul's description of such widows:

> Now she that is a widow indeed, and desolate, trusteth in God, and continueth in supplications and prayers night and day. But she that liveth in pleasure is dead while she liveth (I Tim. 5:5, 6).

Here is the striking contrast between two classes of women. One gives herself to supplications night and day. The other lives in pleasure and is spiritually dead. So

Paul describes a true widow as being great in prayer. Her prayers, born of her faith and desolation, are a mighty force. Day and night her prayers go up to God unceasingly. The widowhood heart is a mighty appeal to God when that heart is found in the way of prayer—intense, unwearied prayer.

One of Paul's striking injunctions worthy of study is this one, "continuing instant in prayer" (see Rom. 12:12), or as the Revised Version reads "be constant in prayer," which is his description of prayer. The term means to tarry, to remain, to be steadfast and faithful in prayer, to stick to it strong, to stay at it with strength to the end, to give attention to it with vigor, devotion and constancy, to give unremitting care to it.

Praying is a business, a life-long business, one to be followed with diligence, fervor, and toil. The Christian's business by way of preeminence is prayer. It is his most engaging, most heavenly, most lucrative business. Prayer is a business of such high and deserved dignity and import that it is to be followed "without ceasing." That is, with no let up nor break down, followed assiduously and without intermission. To prayer we are to give all strength. It must cover all things, be in every place, find itself in all seasons, and embrace everything, always, and everywhere.

In the remarkable prayer in Ephesians 3 Paul is praying for wide reaches of religious experience. He is there bowing his knees unto God in the name of Jesus Christ and asking that God would grant that these Ephesian believers would in their experiences go far beyond the utmost stretches of past sainthood. "Filled with all the fulness of God," an experience so great and so glorious that it makes the head of the modern saint so dizzy that he is afraid to look up to those supernal heights or peer down into the fathomless depths. Paul just passes us on to Him who "is able to do exceeding abundantly above all that we ask or think." This is a specimen of his teaching on prayer.

In writing to the Philippian church, Paul recounts the situation and shows the transmuting power of prayer as follows:

Some indeed preach Christ even of envy and strife; and some also of good will:

The one preach Christ of contention, not sincerely, supposing to add affliction to my bonds:

But the other of love, knowing that I am set for the defence of the gospel.

What then? notwithstanding, every way, whether in pretence, or in truth, Christ is preached; and I therein do rejoice, yea, and will rejoice.

For I know that this shall turn to my salvation through your prayer, and the supply of the Spirit of Jesus Christ.

According to my earnest expectation and my hope, that in nothing I shall be ashamed, but that with all boldness, as always, so now also Christ shall be magnified in my body, whether it be by life or by death (Phil. 1:15-20).

Boldness was to be secured by him and discomfiture and shame prevented by their prayers, and Christ was to be gloriously magnified by and through Paul, whether he lived or died.

It is to be remarked that in all these quotations in Corinthians, Ephesians or Philippians, the Revised Version gives us the most intense form of prayer, "supplications." It is the intense, personal, strenuous, persistent praying of the saints that Paul requests, and they must give special strength, interest, time, and heart to their praying to make it bear its largest golden fruit.

The general direction about prayer to the Colossian

Christians is made specific and is sharpened to the point of a personal appeal: "Continue in prayer, and watch in the same with thanksgiving; Withal praying also for us, that God would open unto us a door of utterance, to speak the mystery of Christ, for which I am also in bonds: That I may make it manifest, as I ought to speak" (Col. 4:2-4).

Paul is accredited with the authorship of the Epistle to the Hebrews. We have it in a reference to the character of Christ's praying, which is illustrative of the elements of true praying. How deep tones are his words! How heart-affecting and how sublime was His praying who prayed as never man prayed before, and yet prayed in order to teach man how to pray, "Who in the days of his flesh, when he had offered up prayers and supplications with strong crying and tears unto him that was able to save him from death, and was heard in that he feared" (Heb. 5:7). The praying of Jesus Christ drew on the mightiest forces of His being. His prayers were His sacrifices, which He offered before He offered Himself on the cross for the sins of mankind. Prayer-sacrifice is the forerunner and pledge of self-sacrifice. We must die in our closets before we can die on the cross.

13
The Necessity for Praying Men

Praying always with all prayer and supplication in the Spirit, and watching thereunto with all perseverance and supplication for all saints.—Ephesians 6:18

Withal praying also for us, that God would open unto us a door of utterance, to speak the mystery of Christ, for which I am also in bonds: That I may make it manifest, as I ought to speak.—Colossians 4:3

One of the crying things of our day is for men whose faith, prayers, and study of the Word of God have been vitalized, and a transcript of that Word is written on their hearts, and who will give it forth as the incorruptible seed that liveth and abideth forever. Nothing more is needed to clear up the haze by which a critical unfaith has eclipsed the Word of God than the fidelity of the pulpit in its unwavering allegiance to the Bible and the fearless proclamation of its truth. Without this

145

the standard bearer fails, and wavering and confusion all along the ranks follow. The pulpit has wrought its mightiest work in the days of its unswerving loyalty to the Word of God.

In close connection with this, must we have men of prayer, men in high and low places who hold to and practice scriptural praying. While the pulpit must hold to its unswerving loyalty to the Word of God, it must, at the same time, be loyal to the doctrine of prayer which that same Word illustrates and enforces upon mankind.

Schools, colleges, and education considered simply as such cannot be regarded as being leaders in carrying forward the work of God's kingdom in the world. They have neither the right, the will, nor the power to do the work. This is to be accomplished by the preached Word, delivered in the power of the Holy Ghost sent down from heaven, sown with prayerful hands and watered with the tears of praying hearts. This is the divine law, and so "nominated in the bond." We are shut up and sealed to it — we would follow the Lord.

Men are demanded for the great work of soul saving, and men must go. It is no angelic or impersonal force which is needed. Human hearts baptized with the spirit of prayer must bear the burden of this message, and human tongues on fire as the result of earnest, persistent prayer, must declare the Word of God to dying men.

The church today needs praying men to execute her solemn and pressing responsibility to meet the fearful crisis which is facing her. The crying need of the times is for men, in increased numbers — God-fearing men, praying men, Holy-Ghost men, men who can endure hardness, who will count not their lives dear unto themselves, but count all things but dross for the excellency of the knowledge of Jesus Christ, the Savior. The men who are so greatly needed in this age of the church are those who have learned the business of praying — learned it upon their knees, learned it in the need and agony of their own hearts.

Praying men are the one commanding need of this day, as of all other days, in which God is to have or make a showing. Men who pray are, in reality, the only religious men, and it takes a full-measured man to pray. Men of prayer are the only men who do or can represent God in this world. No cold, irreligious, prayerless man can claim the right. They misrepresent God in all His work and all His plans. Praying men are the only men who have influence with God, the only kind of men to whom God commits Himself and His gospel. Praying men are the only men in which the Holy Spirit dwells, for the Holy Spirit and prayer go hand-in-hand. The Holy Spirit never descends upon prayerless men. He never fills them, He never empowers them. There is nothing whatever in common between the Spirit of God and men who do not pray. The Spirit dwells only in a prayer atmosphere.

In doing God's work there is no substitute for praying. The men of prayer cannot be displaced with other kinds of men. Men of financial skill, men of education, men of worldly influence — none of these can possibly be put in substitution for the men of prayer. The life, the vigor, the motive power of God's work is formed by praying men. A vitally diseased heart is not a more fearful symptom of approaching death than non-praying men are of spiritual atrophy.

The men to whom Jesus Christ committed the fortunes and destiny of His church were men of prayer. To no other kind of men has God ever committed Himself in this world. The apostles were preeminently men of prayer. They gave themselves to prayer. They make praying their chief business. It was first in point of importance and first in results. God never has, and He never will, commit the weighty interests of His kingdom to prayerless men, who do not make prayer a conspicuous and controlling factor in their lives. Men never rise to any eminence of piety who do not pray. Men of piety are always men of prayer. Men are never noted for the simplicity and strength of their faith who are not preeminently men of prayer. Piety flourishes nowhere so rapidly and so rankly as in the closet. The closet is the garden of faith.

The apostles allowed no duty, however sacred, to so engage them as to infringe upon their time and prevent them from making prayer the main thing. The Word of God was ministered by apostolic fidelity and zeal. It was spoken by men with apostolic commissions and whose heads the fiery tongues of Pentecost had baptized. The Word was pointless and powerless without they were freshly endued with power by continuous and mighty prayer. The seed of God's Word must be saturated in prayer to make it germinate. It grows readier and roots deeper when it is prayer-soaked.

The apostles were praying men themselves. They were teachers of prayer, and trained their disciples in the school of prayer. They urged prayer upon their disciples not only that they might attain to the loftiest eminence of faith, but that they might be the most powerful factors in advancing God's kingdom.

Jesus Christ was the divinely appointed leader of God's people, and no one thing in His life proves His eminent fitness for that office so fully as His habit of prayer. Nothing is more suggestive of thought than Christ's continual praying, and nothing is more conspicuous about Him than prayer. His campaigns were arranged, His victories gained, in the struggles and communion of His all-night praying. His praying rent the heavens. Moses and Elijah and the transfiguration glory waited on His praying. His miracles and His teaching had their force from the same source. Gethsemane's praying crimsoned Calvary with serenity and glory. His prayer makes the history and hastens the triumphs of His church. What an inspiration and command to prayer is Christ's life! What a comment on its worth! How He shames our lives by His praying!

Like all His followers who have drawn God nearer to the world and lifted the world nearer to God, Jesus was the man of prayer, made of God a leader and commander to His people. His leadership was one of prayer. A great leader He was, because He was great in prayer. All great leaders for God have fashioned their leadership in the wrestlings of their closets. Many great men have led and molded the church who have not been great in prayer, but they were great only in their plans, great for their opinions, great for their organization, great by natural gifts, by the force of genius or of character. However, they were not great for God. But Jesus Christ was a great leader for God. His was the great leadership of great praying. God was in His leadership greatly because prayer was in it greatly. We might just well express the wish that we be taught by Him to pray, and to pray more and more.

Herein has been the secret of the men of prayer in the past history of the church. Their hearts were after God, their desires were on Him, their prayers were addressed to Him. They communed with Him, sought nothing of the world, sought great things of God, wrestled with Him, conquered all opposing forces, and opened up the channel of faith deep and broad between them and heaven. And all this was done by the use of prayer. Holy meditations, spiritual desires, heavenly drawings, swayed their intellects, enriched their emotions, and filled and enlarged their hearts. And all this was so because they were first of all men of prayer.

The men who have thus communed with God and who have sought after Him with their whole hearts have always risen to consecrated eminence, and no man has ever risen to this eminence whose flames of holy desire have not all been dead to the world and all aglow for God and heaven. Nor have they ever risen to the heights of the higher spiritual experiences unless prayer and the spirit of prayer have been conspicuous and controlling factors in their lives.

The entire consecration of many of God's children stands out distinctly like towering mountain peaks. Why is this? How did they ascend to these heights? What brought them so near to God? What made them so Christ-like? The answer is easy—prayer. They prayed much, prayed long, and drank deeper and deeper still. They asked, they sought, and they knocked, till heaven opened its richest inner treasures of grace to them. Prayer was the Jacob's ladder by which they scaled those holy and blessed heights, and the way by which the angels of God came down to and ministered to them.

The men of spiritual mold and might always valued prayer. They took time to be alone with God. Their praying was no hurried performance. They had many serious wants to be relieved, and many weighty pleas they had to offer. Many large supplies they must secure. They had to do much silent waiting before God, and much patient iteration and reiteration to utter to Him. Prayer was the only channel through which supplies came and was the only way to utter pleas. The only acceptable waiting before God of which they knew anything was prayer. They valued praying. It was more precious to them than all jewels, more excellent than any good, more to be valued than the greatest good of earth. They esteemed it, valued it, prized it, and did it. They pressed it to its farthest limits, tested its greatest results, and secured its most glorious patrimony. To them prayer was the one great thing to be appreciated and used.

The apostles above everything else were praying men, and left the impress of their prayer example and teaching upon the early church. But the apostles are dead, and times and men have changed. They have no successors by official entail or heirship. And the times have no commission to make other apostles. Prayer is the entail to spiritual and apostolical leadership. Unfortunately the times are not prayerful times. God's cause just now needs very greatly praying leaders. Other things may be needed, but above all else this is the crying demand of these times and the urgent first need of the church.

This is the day of great wealth in the church and of wonderful material resources. But unfortunately the affluence of material resources is a great enemy and a severe hindrance to strong spiritual forces. It is an invariable law that the presence of attractive and potent material forces creates a trust in them and, by the same inevitable law, creates distrust in the spiritual forces of the gospel. They are two masters which cannot be served at one and the same time. For just in proportion as the mind is fixed on one will it be drawn away from the other. The days of great financial prosperity in the church have not been days of great religious prosperity. Moneyed men and praying men are not synonymous terms.

Paul, in the second chapter of his First Epistle to Timothy, emphasizes the need of men to pray. Church leaders in his estimation are to be conspicuous for their praying. Prayer ought and must of necessity shape their characters, and must be one of their distinguishing characteristics. Prayer ought to be one of their most powerful elements, so much so that it cannot be hid. Prayer ought to make church leaders notable. Character, official duty, reputation, and life all should be shaped by prayer. The mighty forces of prayer lie in its praying leaders in a marked way. The standing obligation to pray rests in a peculiar sense on church leaders. Wise will the church be to discover this prime truth and give prominence to it.

It may be laid down as an axiom that God needs, first of all, leaders in the church who will be first in prayer, men with whom prayer is habitual and characteristic, men who know the primacy of prayer. But even more than a habit of prayer, and more than prayer being characteristic of them, church leaders are to be *impregnated* with prayer — men whose lives are made and molded by prayer, whose heart and life are made up of prayer. These are the men — the only men — God can use in the furtherance of His kingdom and the implanting of His message in the hearts of men.

14
The Ministry and Prayer

Of course the preacher is above all others distinguished as a man of prayer. He prays as an ordinary Christian, else he were a hypocrite. He prays more than ordinary Christians else he were disqualified for the office he has undertaken. If you as ministers are not very prayerful you are to be pitied. If you become lax in sacred devotion, not only will you need to be pitied but your people also, and the day cometh in which you will be ashamed and confounded. Our seasons of fastings and prayer at the Tabernacle have been high days indeed; never has heaven's gate stood wider; never have our hearts been nearer the central glory.— Charles H. Spurgeon

Preachers are God's leaders. They are divinely called to their holy office and high purpose and, primarily, are responsible for the condition of the church. Just as Moses was called of God to lead Israel out of Egypt through the wilderness into the Promised Land, so, also, does God call His ministers to lead His spiritual Israel

153

through this world unto the heavenly land. They are divinely commissioned to leadership, and are by precept and example to teach God's people what God would have them be. Paul's counsel to the young preacher Timothy is in point: "Let no man despise thy youth," he says, "but be thou an example of the believers, in word, in conversation, in charity, in spirit, in faith, in purity" (I Tim. 4:12).

God's ministers shape the church's character, and give tone and direction to its life. The prefacing sentence of the letter to each of the seven churches in Asia reads, "To the angel of the church," seeming to indicate that the angel—the minister—was in the same state of mind and condition of life as the membership and that these "angels" or ministers were largely responsible for the spiritual condition of things existing in each church. The "angel" in each case was the preacher, teacher, or leader. The first Christians knew full well and felt this responsibility. In their helplessness, consciously felt, they cried out, "And who is sufficient for these things?" as the tremendous responsibility pressed upon their hearts and heads. The only reply to such a question was, "God only." So they were necessarily compelled to look beyond themselves for help and throw themselves on prayer to secure God. More and more as they prayed did they feel their responsibility, and more and more by prayer did they get God's help. They realized that their sufficiency was of God.

Prayer belongs in a very high and important sense to the ministry. It takes vigor and elevation of character to administer the prayer office. Praying prophets have frequently been at a premium in the history of God's people. In every age the demand has been for leaders in Israel who pray. God's watchmen must always and everywhere be men of prayer.

It ought to be no surprise for ministers to be often

found on their knees seeking divine help under the responsibility of their call. These are the true prophets of the Lord, and these are they who stand as mouthpieces of God to a generation of wicked and worldly-minded men and women. Praying preachers are boldest, the truest and the swiftest ministers of God. They mount up highest and are nearest to Him who has called them. They advance more rapidly and in Christian living are most like God.

In reading the record of the four evangelists, we cannot but be impressed by the supreme effort made by our Lord to rightly instruct the twelve apostles in the things which would properly qualify them for the tremendous tasks which would be theirs after He had gone back to the bosom of the Father. His solicitude was for the church that she should have men, holy in life and in heart, and who would know full well from whence came their strength and power in the work of the ministry. A large part of Christ's teaching was addressed to these chosen apostles, and the training of the twelve occupied much of His thought and consumed much of His time. In all that training, prayer was laid down as a basic principle.

We find the same thing to be true in the life and work of the apostle Paul. While he addressed himself to the edification of the churches to whom he ministered and wrote, it was in his mind and purpose to rightly instruct and prepare ministers to whom would be committed the interests of God's people. The two epistles to Timothy were addressed to a young preacher, while that to Titus was also written to a young minister. And Paul's design appears to have been to give to each of them such instruction as would be needed rightly to do the work of the ministry to which they had been called by the Spirit of God. Underlying these instructions was the foundation stone of prayer, since by no means would they be able to "show themselves approved unto God, workmen that needeth not to be ashamed, rightly dividing the word of truth" (see II Tim. 2:15) unless they were men of prayer.

The highest welfare of the church of God on earth depends largely upon the ministry, and so almighty God has always been jealous of His watchmen — His preachers. His concern has been for the character of the men who minister at His altars in holy things. They must be men who lean upon Him, who look to Him, and who continually seek Him for wisdom, help, and power effectively to do the work of the ministry. And so He has designed men of prayer for the holy office and has relied upon them successively to perform the tasks He has assigned them.

God's great works are to be done as Christ did them; are to be done, indeed, with increased power received from the ascended and exalted Christ. These works are to be done by prayer. Men must do God's work in God's way, and to God's glory, and prayer is a necessity to its successful accomplishment.

The thing far above all other things in the equipment of the preacher is prayer. Before everything else, he must be a man who makes a specialty of prayer. A prayerless preacher is a misnomer. He has either missed his calling, or has grievously failed God who called him into the ministry. God wants men who are not ignoramuses, who "study to show themselves approved." Preaching the Word is essential; social qualities are not to be underestimated, and education is good; but under and above all else, prayer must be the main plank in the platform of the man who goes forth to preach the unsearchable riches of Christ to a lost and hungry world. The one weak spot in our church institutions lies just here. Prayer is not regarded as being the primary factor in church life and activity, and other things, good in their places, are made primary. First things need to be put first, and the first thing in the equipment of a minister is prayer.

Our Lord is the pattern for all preachers, and, with Him, prayer was the law of life. By it He lived. It was the inspiration of His toil, the source of His strength, the spring of His joy. With our Lord prayer was no sentimental episode, nor an afterthought, nor a pleasing, diverting prelude, nor an interlude, nor a parade or form. For Jesus, prayer was exacting, all-absorbing, paramount. It was the call of a sweet duty to Him, the satisfying of a restless yearning, the preparation for heavy responsibilities, and the meeting of a vigorous need. This being so, the disciple must be as His Lord, the servant as his Master. As was the Lord Himself, so also must be those whom He has called to be His disciples. Our Lord Jesus Christ chose His twelve apostles only after He had spent a night in praying; and we may rest assured that He sets the same high value on those He calls to His ministry, in this our own day and time.

No feeble or secondary place was given to prayer in the ministry of Jesus. It comes first — emphatic, conspicuous, controlling. Of prayerful habits, of a prayerful spirit, given to long solitary communion with God, Jesus was above all else, a man of prayer. The crux of His earthly history, in New Testament terminology, is condensed to a single statement, to be found in Hebrews 5:7:

Who in the days of his flesh, when he had offered up prayers and supplications with strong crying and tears unto him that was able to save him from death, and was heard in that he feared.

As was their Lord and Master, whose they are and whom they serve, so let His ministers be. Let Him be their pattern, their example, their leader and teacher.

Much reference is made in some quarters about "following Christ," but it is confined to the following of Him in modes and ordinances, as if salvation were wrapped up in the specific way of doing a thing. "The path of prayer thyself hath trod," is the path along which we are to follow Him, and in no other. Jesus was given as a leader to the people of God, and no leader ever exemplified more the worth and necessity of prayer. Equal in glory with the Father, anointed and sent on His special mission by the Holy Spirit, His incarnate birth, His high commission, His royal anointing — all these were His but they did not relieve Him from the exacting claims of prayer. Rather did they tend to impose these claims upon Him with greater authority. He did not ask to be excused from the burden of prayer; he gladly accepted it, acknowledged its claims and voluntarily subjected Himself to its demands.

His leadership was preeminent, and His praying was preeminent. Had it not been, His leadership had been neither preeminent nor divine. If, in true leadership, prayer had been dispensable, then certainly Jesus could have dispensed with it. But He did not, nor can any of His followers who desire effectiveness in Christian activity do other than follow their Lord.

While Jesus Christ practiced praying Himself, being personally under the law of prayer, and while His parables and miracles were but exponents of prayer, He labored directly to teach His disciples the specific art of praying. He said little or nothing about how to preach or what to preach. But He spent His strength and time in teaching men how to speak to God, how to commune with Him, and how to be with Him. He knew full well that he who has learned the craft of talking to God will be well versed in talking to men. We may turn aside for a moment to observe that this was the secret of the wonderful success of the early Methodist preachers, who were far from being learned men. But with all their limitations, they were men of prayer, and they did great things for God.

All ability to talk to men is measured by the ability with which a preacher can talk to God for men. He "who ploughs not in his closet, will never reap in his pulpit."

The fact must ever be kept in the forefront and emphasized that Jesus Christ trained His disciples to pray. This is the real meaning of that saying, "The Training of the Twelve." It must be kept in mind that Christ taught the world's preachers more about praying than He did about preaching. Prayer was the great factor in the spreading of His gospel. Prayer conserved and made efficient all other factors. Yet He did not discount preaching when He stressed praying, but rather taught the utter dependence of preaching on prayer.

"The Christian's trade is praying," declared Martin Luther. Every Jewish boy had to learn a trade. Jesus Christ learned two, the trade of a carpenter and that of praying. The one trade subserved earthly uses; the other served His divine and higher purposes. Jewish custom committed Jesus when a boy to the trade of a carpenter; the law of God bound Him to praying from His earliest years and remained with Him to the end.

Christ is the Christian's example, and every Christian must pattern after Him. Every preacher must be like His Lord and Master and must learn the trade of praying. He who learns well the trade of praying masters the secret of the Christian art and becomes a skilled workman in God's workshop, one who needeth not to be ashamed, a worker together with his Lord and Master.

"Pray without ceasing," is the trumpet call to the preachers of our time. If the preachers will get their thoughts clothed with the atmosphere of prayer, if they will prepare their sermons on their knees, a gracious outpouring of God's Spirit will come upon the earth.

The one indispensable qualification for preaching is the gift of the Holy Spirit, and it was for the bestowal of this indispensable gift that the disciples were charged to tarry in Jerusalem. The absolute necessity there is for receiving this gift if success is to attend the efforts of the ministry, is found in the command the first disciples had to stay in Jerusalem till they received it, and also with the instant and earnest prayerfulness with which they sought it. In obedience to their Lord's command to tarry in that city till they were endued with power from on high, they immediately, after He left them for heaven, entered on securing it by continued and earnest prayer. "These all continued with one accord in prayer and supplication, with the women, and Mary the mother of Jesus, and with his brethren" (Acts 1:14). To this same thing John refers in his First Epistle. "Ye have an unction from the Holy One," he says. It is this divine unction that preachers of the present day should sincerely desire, pray for, remaining unsatisfied till the blessed gift be richly bestowed.

Another allusion to this same important procedure is made by our Lord shortly after His resurrection, when He said to His disciples: "But ye shall receive power, after that the Holy Ghost is come upon you" (Acts 1:8a). At the same time Jesus directed the attention of His disciples to the statement of John the Baptist concerning the Spirit, the identical thing for which He had commanded them to tarry in the city of Jerusalem—"power from on high." Alluding to John the Baptist's words Jesus said, "For John truly baptized with water; but ye shall be baptized with the Holy Ghost not many days hence" (Acts 1:5). Peter at a later date said of our Lord: "God anointed him with the Holy Ghost and with power."

These are the divine statements of the mission and ministry of the Holy Spirit to preachers of that day and the same divine statements apply with equal force to the preachers of *this* day. God's ideal minister is a God-called, divinely-anointed, Spirit-touched man, separated unto God's work, set apart from secularities and questionable affairs, baptized from above, marked, sealed and owned by the Spirit, devoted to his Master and His ministry. These are the divinely-appointed requisites for a preacher of the Word; without them, he is inadequate and inevitably unfruitful.

Today, there is no dearth of preachers who deliver eloquent sermons on the need and nature of revival, and advance elaborate plans for the spread of the kingdom of God, but the praying preachers are far more rare and the greatest benefactor this age can have is a man who will bring the preachers, the church, and the people back to the practice of real praying. The reformer needed just now is the praying reformer. The leader Israel requires is one who, with clarion voice, will call the ministry back to their knees.

There is considerable talk of the coming revival in the air, but we need to have the vision to see that the revival we need and the only one that can be worth having is one that is born of the Holy Spirit, which brings deep conviction for sin, and regeneration for those who seek God's face. Such a revival comes at the end of a season of real praying, and it is utter folly to talk about or expect a revival without the Holy Spirit operating in His peculiar office, conditioned on much earnest praying. Such a revival will begin in pulpit and pew alike, will be promoted by both preacher and layman working in harmony with God.

The heart is the lexicon of prayer; the life the best commentary on prayer, and the outward bearing its fullest expression. The character is made by prayer; the life is perfected by prayer. And this the ministry needs to learn as thoroughly as the laymen. There is but one rule for both.

So averse was the general body of Christ's disciples to prayer, having so little taste for it, and having so little sympathy with Him in the deep things of prayer and its mightier struggles, that the Master had to select a circle of three more apt scholars—Peter, James, and John—who had more of sympathy and relish for this divine work, and take them aside that they might learn the lesson of prayer. These men were nearer to Jesus, fuller of sympathy, and more helpful to Him because they were more prayerful.

Blessed, indeed, are those disciples whom Jesus Christ, in this day, calls into a more intimate fellowship with Him, and who, readily responding to the call, are found much on their knees before Him. Distressing, indeed, is the condition of those servants of Jesus who, in their hearts, are averse to the exercise of the ministry of prayer.

All the great eras of our Lord, historical and spiritual, were made or fashioned by His praying. In like manner His plans and great achievements were born in prayer and impregnated by the spirit thereof. As was the Master, so also must His servant be; as his Lord did in the great eras of His life, so should the disciple do when faced by important crises. "To your knees, O Israel!" should be the clarion call to the ministry of this generation.

The highest form of religious life is attained by prayer. The richest revelations of God—Father, Son, and Spirit—are made, not to the learned, the great, or the "noble" of earth, but men of prayer. "For ye see your calling, brethren, how that not many wise men after the flesh, not many mighty, not many noble, are called" (I Cor. 1:26), to whom God makes known the deep things of God and reveals the higher things of His character, but to the lowly, inquiring, praying ones. And again must it be said, this is as true of preachers as of laymen. It is the spiritual man who prays, and to praying ones God makes His revelations through the Holy Spirit.

Praying preachers have always brought the greater glory to God, have moved His gospel onward with its greatest, speediest rate and power. A non-praying preacher and a non-praying church may flourish outwardly and advance in many aspects of their life. Both preacher and church may become synonyms for success, but unless it rest on a praying basis all success will eventually crumble into deadened life and ultimate decay.

"Ye have not because ye ask not," is the solution of all spiritual weakness both in the personal life and in the pulpit. Either that or it is, "Ye ask and receive not because ye ask amiss." Real praying lies at the foundation of all real success of the ministry in the things of God. The stability, energy, and facility with which God's kingdom is established in this world are dependent upon prayer. God has made it so, and so God is anxious for men to pray. Especially is He concerned that His chosen ministers shall be men of prayer, and so gives that wonderful statement in order to encourage His ministers to pray, which is found in Matthew 7:7, 8:

> Ask, and it shall be given you; seek, and ye shall find; knock, and it shall be opened unto you. For every one that asketh receiveth, and he that seeketh findeth; and to him that knocketh it shall be opened.

Thus both command and direct promise give accent to His concern that they shall pray. Pause and think on these familiar words. "Ask, and it shall be given you." That itself would seem to be enough to set us all, laymen and preachers, to praying, so direct, simple, and unlimited. These words open all the treasures of heaven to us, simply by asking for them.

If we have not studied the prayers of Paul, primarily a preacher to the Gentiles, we can have but a feeble view of the great necessity for prayer and how much it is worth in the life and the work of a minister of the gospel. Furthermore, we shall have but a very limited view of the possibilities of the gospel to enrich and make strong and perfect Christian character, as well as to equip preachers for their high and holy task. Oh, when will we learn the simple yet all important lesson that the one great thing needed in the life of a preacher to help him in his personal life, to keep his soul alive to God, and to give efficacy to the Word preached by him, is real, constant prayer!

Paul, with prayer uppermost in his mind, assures the Colossians that "Epaphras . . . is always labouring fervently for you in prayers, that ye may stand complete and perfect in all the will of God" (Col. 4:12). To this high state of grace, "complete in all the will of God," he prays they may come. So prayer was the force which was to bring them to that elevated, vigorous, and stable state of heart. This is in line with Paul's teaching to the Ephesians, "And he gave some . . . pastors and teachers; For the perfecting of the saints, for the work of the ministry, for the edifying of the body of Christ" (Eph. 4:11, 12), where it is evidently affirmed that the whole work of the ministry is not merely to induce sinners to repent, but it is also the "perfecting of the saints." And so Epaphras "laboured fervently in prayers" for this thing. Certainly he was himself a praying man, in thus so earnestly praying for these early Christians.

The apostles put out their force in order that Christians should honor God by the purity and consistency of their outward lives. They were to reproduce the character of Jesus Christ. They were to perfect His image in themselves, imbibe His temper, and reflect His carriage in all their tempers and conduct. They were to be imitators of God as dear children, to be holy as He was holy. Thus even laymen were to preach by their conduct and character, just as the ministry preached with their mouths.

To elevate the followers of Christ to these exalted heights of Christian experience, they were in every way true in the ministry of God's Word, in the ministry of prayer, in holy consuming zeal, in burning exhortation, in rebuke and reproof. Added to all these, sanctifying all these, invigorating all these, and making all of them salutary, they centered and exercised constantly the force of mightiest praying. "Night and day praying exceedingly," that is, praying out of measure, with intense earnestness, superabundantly, beyond measure, exceeding abundantly.

> Night and day praying exceedingly that we might see your face, and might perfect that which is lacking in your faith? Now God himself and our Father, and our Lord Jesus Christ, direct our way unto you.

> And the Lord make you to increase and abound in love one toward another, and toward all men, even as we do toward you; To the end he may stablish your hearts unblameable in holiness before God, even our Father, at the coming of our Lord Jesus Christ with all his saints (I Thess. 3:10-13).

It was after this fashion that these apostles — the first preachers in the early church — labored in prayer. And only those who labor after the same fashion are the true successors of these apostles. This is the true, the scriptural "apostolical succession," the succession of simple faith, earnest desire for holiness of heart and life, and zealous praying. These are the things today which make the ministry strong, faithful, and efficient, "workmen who needeth not to be ashamed, rightly dividing the word of truth" (see II Tim. 2:15).

Jesus Christ, God's leader and commander of His people, lived and suffered under this law of prayer. All His personal conquests in His life on earth were won by obedience to this law, while the conquests which have been won by His representatives since He ascended to heaven were gained only when this condition of prayer was heartily and fully met. Christ was under this one prayer condition. His apostles were under the same prayer condition. His saints are under it, and even His angels are under it. By every token, therefore, preachers are under the same prayer law. Not for one moment are they relieved or excused from obedience to the law of prayer. It is their very life, the source of their power, the secret of their religious experience and communion with God.

Christ could do nothing without prayer. Christ could do all things by prayer. The apostles were helpless without prayer—and were absolutely dependent upon it for success in defeating their spiritual foes. They could do all things by prayer.

Excerpts from

The Reality of Prayer

Prayer — A Privilege, Princely, Sacred
Jesus Christ, the Divine Teacher of Prayer
Our Lord's Model Prayer

15

Prayer — a Privilege, Princely, Sacred

I am the creature of a day, passing through life as an arrow through the air. I am a spirit come from God and returning to God; just hovering over the great gulf; till a few moments hence I am no more seen; I drop into an unchangeable eternity! I want to know one thing, the way to heaven; how to land safe on that happy shore. God Himself has condescended to teach the way; for this end He came from heaven. He hath written it down in a book. O give me that book! At any price give me the Book of God! Lord, is it not Thy word—"If any man lack wisdom, let him ask of God? Thou givest liberally, and upbraidest not. Thou hast said, if any be willing to do Thy will he shall know. I am willing to do; let me know Thy will."—John Wesley

The word "prayer" expresses the largest and most comprehensive approach unto God. It gives prominence to the element of devotion. It is communion and intercourse with God. It is enjoyment of God. It is access to

169

God. "Supplication" is a more restricted and more intense form of prayer, accompanied by a sense of personal need, limited to the seeking in an urgent manner of a supply for pressing need.

"Supplication" is the very soul of prayer in the way of pleading for some one thing, greatly needed and the need intensely felt.

"Intercession" is an enlargement in prayer, a going out in broadness and fullness from self to others. Primarily, it does not center in praying for others, but refers to the freeness, boldness, and childlike confidence of the praying. It is the fullness of confiding influence in the soul's approach to God, unlimited and unhesitating in its access and its demands. This influence and confident trust is to be used for others.

Prayer always and everywhere is an immediate and confiding approach to, and a request of, God the Father. In the prayer universal and perfect, as the pattern of all praying, it is "Our Father which art in heaven." At the grave of Lazarus, Jesus lifted up His eyes and said, "Father." In His sacerdotal prayer, Jesus lifted up His eyes to heaven, and said, "Father." Personal, familiar, and paternal was all His praying. Strong, too, and touching and tearful, was His praying. Read these words of Paul: "Who in the days of his flesh, when he had offered up prayers and supplications with strong crying and tears unto him that was able to save him from death, and was heard in that he feared" (Heb. 5:7).

So elsewhere (James 1:5) we have "asking" set forth as prayer: "If any of you lack wisdom, let him ask of God, who giveth to all men liberally, and upbraideth not; and it shall be given him."

"Asking of God" and "receiving" from the Lord — direct application to God, immediate connection with God — that is prayer.

In I John 5:14 and 15 we have this statement about prayer:

> And this is the confidence that we have in him, that, if we ask any thing according to his will, he heareth us: And if we know that he hear us, whatsoever we ask, we know that we have the petitions that we desired of him.

In Philippians 4:6 we have these words about prayer:

> Be careful for nothing; but in every thing, by prayer and supplication with thanksgiving let your requests be made known unto God.

What is God's will about prayer? First of all, it is God's will that we pray. Jesus Christ "spake a parable unto them to this end, that men ought always to pray, and not to faint" (Luke 18:1).

Paul writes to young Timothy about the first things which God's people are to do, and first among the first he puts prayer: "I exhort therefore, that, first of all, supplications, prayers, intercessions, and giving of thanks, be made for all men" (I Tim. 2:1).

In connection with these words Paul declares that the will of God and the redemption and mediation of Jesus Christ for the salvation for all men are all vitally concerned in this matter of prayer. In this his apostolical authority and solicitude of soul conspire with God's will and Christ's intercession to will that "the men pray everywhere."

Note how frequently prayer is brought forward in the New Testament: "Continuing instant in prayer"; "Pray without ceasing"; "Continue in prayer, and watch in the same with thanksgiving"; "Be ye sober and watch unto prayer." Christ's clarion call was "watch and pray." What are all these and others if it is not the will of God that men should pray?

Prayer is complement, made efficient and cooperate with God's will, whose sovereign sway is to run parallel in extent and power with the atonement of Jesus Christ. He through the eternal Spirit, by the grace of God, "tasted death for every man." We, through the eternal Spirit, by the grace of God, *pray* for every man.

But how do I know that I am praying by the will of God? Every true attempt to pray is in response to the will of God. Bungling it may be and untutored by human teachers, but it is acceptable to God, because it is in obedience to His will. If I will give myself up to the inspiration of the Spirit of God, who commands me to pray, the details and the petitions of that praying will all fall into harmony with the will of Him who wills that I should pray.

Prayer is no little thing, no selfish and small matter. It does not concern the petty interests of one person. The littlest prayer broadens out by the will of God till it touches all words, conserves all interests, and enhances man's greatest wealth, and God's greatest good. God is so concerned that men pray that He has promised to answer prayer. He has not promised to do something general if we pray, but He has promised to do the very thing for which we pray.

Prayer, as taught by Jesus in its essential features, enters into all the relations of life. It sanctifies brotherliness. To the Jew, the altar was the symbol and place of prayer. The Jew devoted the altar to the worship of God. Jesus Christ takes the altar of prayer and devotes it to the worship of the brotherhood. How Christ purifies the altar and enlarges it! How He takes it out of the sphere of a mere performance and makes its virtue to consist not in the mere act of praying, but in the spirit which actuates us toward men. Our spirit toward folks is of the life of prayer. We must be at peace with men, and, if possible, have them at peace with us before we can be at peace with God. Reconciliation with men is the forerunner of reconciliation with God. Our spirit and words must embrace men before they can embrace God. Unity with the brotherhood goes before unity with God. "Therefore if thou bring thy gift to the altar, and there rememberest that thy brother hath aught against thee; Leave there thy gift before the altar, and go thy way; first be reconciled to thy brother, and then come and offer thy gift" (Matt. 5:23, 24).

Non-praying is lawlessness, discord, anarchy. Prayer, in the moral government of God, is as strong and far-reaching as the law of gravitation in the material world, and it is as necessary as gravitation to hold things in their proper sphere and in life.

The space occupied by prayer in the Sermon on the Mount bespeaks its estimate by Christ and the importance it holds in His system. Many important principles are discussed in a verse or two. The Sermon consists of 111 verses, and 18 are about prayer directly, and others indirectly.

Prayer was one of the cardinal principles of piety in every dispensation and to every child of God. It did not pertain to the business of Christ to originate duties, but to recover, to recast, to spiritualize, and to re-enforce those duties which are cardinal and original.

With Moses the great features of prayer are prominent. He never beats the air nor fights a sham battle. The most serious and strenuous business of his serious and strenuous life was prayer. He is much at it with the intensest earnestness of his soul. Intimate as he was with God, his intimacy did not abate the necessity of prayer. This intimacy only brought clearer insight into the nature and necessity of prayer, and led him to see the greater obligations to pray, and to discover the larger results of praying. In reviewing one of the crises through which Israel passed, when the very existence of the nation was imperilled, he writes: "I fell down before the Lord forty days and forty nights." Wonderful praying and wonderful results! Moses knew how to do wonderful praying, and God knew how to give wonderful results.

The whole force of Bible statement is to increase our faith in the doctrine that prayer affects God, secures favors from God, which can be secured in no other way, and which will not be bestowed by God if we do not pray. The whole canon of Bible teaching is to illustrate the great truth that God hears and answers prayer. One of the great purposes of God in His Book is to impress upon us indelibly the great importance, the priceless value, and the absolute necessity of asking God for the things which we need for time and eternity. He urges us by every consideration and presses and warns us by every interest. He points us to His own Son, turned over to us for our good, as His pledge that prayer will be answered, teaching us that God is our Father, able to do all things for us and to give all things to us, much more than earthly parents are able or willing to do for their children.

Let us thoroughly understand ourselves and understand also this great business of prayer. Our one great business is prayer, and we will never do it well without we fasten to it by all binding force. We will never do it well without arranging the best conditions of doing it well. Satan has suffered so much by good praying that all his wily, shrewd, and ensnaring devices will be used to cripple its performances.

We must, by all the fastenings we can find, cable ourselves to prayer. To be loose in time and place is to open the door to Satan. To be exact, prompt, unswerving, and careful in even the little things, is to buttress ourselves against the evil one.

Prayer, by God's very oath, is put in the very stones of God's foundations, as eternal as its companion, "And men shall pray for him continually." This is the eternal condition which advances His cause and makes it powerfully aggressive. Men are always to pray for it. Its strength, beauty, and aggression lie in their prayers. Its power lies simply in its power to pray. No power is found elsewhere but in its ability to pray. "For my house shall be called the house of prayer for all people." It is based on prayer and carried on by the same means.

Prayer is a privilege, a sacred, princely privilege. Prayer is a duty, an obligation most binding and most imperative which should hold us to it. But prayer is more than a privilege, more than a duty. It is a means, an instrument, a condition. Not to pray is to lose much more than to fail in the exercise and enjoyment of a high or sweet privilege. Not to pray is to fail along lines far more important than even the violation of an obligation.

Prayer is the appointed condition of getting God's aid. This aid is as manifold and illimitable as God's ability and as varied and exhaustless is this aid as man's need. Prayer is the avenue through which God supplies man's wants. Prayer is the channel through which all good flows from God to man, and all good from men to men. God is the Christian's father. Asking and giving are in that relation.

Man is the one more immediately concerned in this great work of praying. It ennobles man's reason to employ it in prayer. The office and work of prayer is the divinest engagement of man's reason. Prayer makes man's reason to shine. Intelligence of the highest order approves prayer. He is the wisest man who prays the most and the best. Prayer is the school of wisdom as well as of piety.

Prayer is not a picture to handle, to admire, to look at. It is not beauty, coloring, shape, attitude, imagination, or genius. These things do not pertain to its character or conduct. It is not poetry nor music. Its inspiration and melody come from heaven. Prayer belongs to the spirit, and at times it possesses the spirit and stirs the spirit with high and holy purposes and resolves.

16
Jesus Christ, the Divine Teacher of Prayer

A friend of mine in his journey is come to me, and I have nothing to set before him! He knocks again. "Friend! lend me three loaves." He waits a while and then knocks again. "Friend! I must have three loaves!" "Trouble me not: the door is now shut; I cannot rise and give thee!" He stands still. He turns to go home. He comes back. He knocks again. "Friend!" he cries. He puts his ear to the door. There is a sound inside, and then the light of a candle shines through the hole of the door. The bars of the door are drawn back, and he gets not three loaves only, but as many as he needs. "And I say unto you, Ask and it shall be given you; seek and ye shall find; knock and it shall be opened unto you."—Alexander Whyte

Jesus Christ was the divine teacher of prayer. Its power and nature had been illustrated by many a saint and prophet in olden times, but modern sainthood and modern teachers of prayer had lost their inspiration and life. Religiously dead teachers and superficial ecclesiastics had forgotten what it was to pray. They did much of saying prayers, on state occasions, in public, with much ostentation and parade, but pray they did not. To them it was almost a lost practice. In the multiplicity of saying prayers they had lost the art of praying.

The history of the disciples during the earthly life of our Lord was not marked with much devotion. They were much enamored by their personal association with Christ. They were charmed by His words, excited by His miracles, and were entertained and concerned by the hopes which a selfish interest aroused in His person and mission. Taken up with the superficial and worldly views of His character, they neglected and overlooked the deeper and weightier things which belonged to Him and His mission. The neglect of the most obliging and ordinary duties by them was a noticeable feature in their conduct. So evident and singular was their conduct in this regard that it became a matter of grave inquiry on one occasion and severe chiding on another.

"And they said unto him, Why do the disciples of John fast often, and make prayers, and likewise the disciples of the Pharisees; but thine eat and drink? And he said unto them, Can ye make the children of the bridechamber fast, while the bridegroom is with them? But the days will come, when the bridegroom shall be taken away from them, and then shall they fast in those days" (Luke 5:33-35).

In the example and the teaching of Jesus Christ, prayer assumes its normal relation to God's person, God's movements, and God's Son. Jesus Christ was essentially the teacher of prayer by precept and example. We have glimpses of His praying which, like indices, tell how full of prayer the pages, chapters, and volumes of His life were. The epitome which covers not one segment only, but the whole circle of His life, and character, is preeminently that of prayer! "In the days of his flesh," the divine record reads "when he had offered up prayers and supplications with strong crying and tears." The suppliant of all suppliants He was, the intercessor of all intercessors. In lowliest form He approached God, and with strongest pleas He prayed and supplicated.

Jesus Christ teaches the importance of prayer by His urgency to His disciples to pray. But He shows us more than that. He shows how far prayer enters into the purposes of God. We must ever keep in mind that the relation of Jesus Christ to God is the relation of asking and giving, the Son ever asking, the Father ever giving. We must never forget that God has put the conquering, inheriting, and expanding forces of Christ's cause in prayer. "Ask of me, and I shall give thee the heathen for thine inheritance, and the uttermost parts of the earth for thy possession" (Ps. 2:8).

This was the clause embodying the royal proclamation and the universal condition when the Son was enthroned as the world's mediator, and when He was sent on His mission of receiving grace and power. We very naturally learn from this how Jesus would stress praying as the one sole condition of His receiving His possession and inheritance.

Necessarily in this study on prayer, lines of thought will cross each other, and the same Scripture passage or incident will be mentioned more than once, simply because a passage may teach one or more truths. This is the case when we speak of the vast comprehensiveness of prayer. How all-inclusive Jesus Christ makes prayer! It has no limitations in extent or things! The promises to prayer are godlike in their magnificence, wideness, and universality. In their nature these promises have to do with God—with Him in their inspiration, creation, and results. Who but God could say, "And all things, whatsoever ye shall ask in prayer, believing, ye shall receive" (Matt 21:22)? Who can command and direct "all things whatsoever" but God? Neither man nor chance nor the law of results are so far lifted above change, limitations or condition, nor have in them mighty forces which can direct and result all things, as to promise the bestowment and direction of all things.

Whole sections, parables, and incidents were used by Christ to enforce the necessity and importance of prayer. His miracles are but parables of prayer. In nearly all of them prayer figures distinctly, and some features of it are illustrated. The Syrophoenician woman is a preeminent illustration of the ability and the success of importunity in prayer. The case of blind Bartimaeus has points of suggestion along the same line. Jairus and the centurion illustrate and impress phases of prayer. The parable of the Pharisee and the publican enforce humility in prayer, declare the wondrous results of praying, and show the vanity and worthlessness of wrong praying. The failure to enforce church discipline and the readiness of violating the brotherhood, are all used to make an exhibit of far-reaching results of agreed praying, a record of which we have in Matthew 18:19.

It is of prayer in concert that Christ is speaking. Two agreed ones, two whose hearts have been keyed into perfect symphony by the Holy Spirit. Anything that they shall ask, it shall be done. Christ had been speaking of discipline in the church, how things were to be kept in unity, and how the fellowship of the brethren was to be maintained, by the restoration of the offender or by his exclusion. Members who had been true to the brotherhood of Christ, and who were laboring to preserve that brotherhood unbroken, would be the agreed ones to make appeals to God in united prayer.

In the Sermon on the Mount, Christ lays down constitutional principles. Types and shadows are retired, and the law of spiritual life is declared. In this foundation law of the Christian system prayer assumes a conspicuous, if not a paramount, position. It is not only wide, all-commanding, and comprehensive in its own sphere of action and relief, but it is ancillary to all duties. Even the one demanding kindly and discriminating judgment toward others, and also the royal injunction, the golden rule of action, these owe their being to prayer.

Christ puts prayer among the statutory promises. He does not leave it to natural law. The law of need, demand and supply, of helplessness, of natural instincts, or the law of sweet, high, attractive privilege—these howsoever strong as motives of action are not the basis of praying. Christ puts it as spiritual law. Men must pray. Not to pray is not simply a privation, an omission, but a positive violation of law, of spiritual life, a crime, bringing disorder and ruin. Prayer is law world-wide and eternity-reaching.

In the Sermon on the Mount many important utterances are dismissed with a line or a verse, while the subject of prayer occupies a large space. To it Christ returns again and again. He bases the possibilities and necessities of prayer on the relation of father and child, the child crying for bread, and the father giving that for which the child asks. Prayer and its answer are in the relation of a father to his child. The teaching of Jesus Christ on the nature and necessity of prayer as recorded in His life, is remarkable. He sends men to their closets. Prayer must be a holy exercise, untainted by vanity or pride. It must be in secret. The disciple must live in secret. God lives there, is sought there, and is found there. The command of Christ as to prayer is that pride and publicity should be shunned. Prayer is to be in private. "But thou, when thou prayest, enter into thy closet, and when thou hast shut thy door, pray to thy Father which is in secret; and thy Father which seeth in secret shall reward thee openly" (Matt. 6:6).

The Beatitudes are not only to enrich and adorn, but they are the material out of which spiritual character is built. The very first one of these fixes prayer in the very foundation of spiritual character, not simply to adorn, but to compose. "Blessed are the poor in spirit." The word "poor" means a pauper, one who lives by begging. The real Christian lives on the bounties of another, whose bounties he gets by asking. Prayer then becomes the basis of Christian character, the Christian's business, his life, and his living. This is Christ's law of prayer, putting it into the very being of the Christian. It is his first step, and his first breath, which is to color and to form all his after life. Blessed are the poor ones, for they only can pray.

> Prayer is the Christian's vital breath,
> The Christian's native air;
> His watchword at the gates of death;
> He enters Heaven with prayer.

From praying Christ eliminates all self-sufficiency, all pride, and all spiritual values. The poor in spirit are the praying ones. Beggars are God's princes. They are God's heirs. Christ removes the rubbish of Jewish traditions and glosses from the regulations of the prayer altar.

Ye have heard that it was said by them of old time, Thou shalt not kill; and whosoever shall kill shall be in danger of the judgment:

But I say unto you, That whosoever is angry with his brother shall be in danger of the judgment: and whosoever shall say to his brother, Raca, shall be in danger of the council: but whosoever shall say, Thou fool, shall be in danger of hell fire.

Therefore if thou bring thy gift to the altar, and there rememberest that thy brother hath ought against thee;

Leave there thy gift before the altar, and go thy way; first, be reconciled to thy brother, and then come and offer thy gift (Matt. 5:21-24).

He who essays to pray to God with an angry spirit, with loose and irreverent lips, with an irreconciled heart, and with unsettled neighborly scores, spends his labor for that which is worse than naught, violates the law of prayer, and adds to his sin.

How rigidly exacting is Christ's law of prayer! It goes to the heart and demands that love be enthroned there, love to the brotherhood. The sacrifice of prayer must be seasoned and perfumed with love, by love in the inward parts. The law of prayer, its creator and inspirer, is love.

Praying must be done. God wants it done. He commands it. Man needs it and man must do it. Something must surely come of praying, for God engages that something shall come out of it if men are in earnest and are persevering in prayer.

After Jesus teaches "Ask and it shall be given you," etc., He encourages real praying and more praying. He repeats and avers with redoubled assurance, "For every one that asketh receiveth." No exception. "Every one." "He that seeketh, findeth." Here it is again, sealed and stamped with infinite veracity. Then closed and signed, as well as sealed, with divine attestation, "To him that knocketh it shall be opened." Note how we are encouraged to pray by our relation to God!

If ye then, being evil, know how to give good gifts unto your children, how much more shall your Father which is in heaven give good things to them that ask him (Matt. 7:11).

The relation of prayer to God's work and God's rule in this world is most fully illustrated by Jesus Christ in both His teaching and His practice. He is first in every way and in everything. Among the rulers of the church He is primary in a preeminent way. He has the throne. The golden crown is His in eminent preciousness. The white garments enrobe Him in preeminent whiteness and beauty. In the ministry of prayer He is a divine example as well as the divine teacher. His example is affluent, and His prayer teaching abounds. How imperative the teaching of our Lord when He affirms that "men ought always to pray and not to faint!" and then presents a striking parable of an unjust judge and a poor widow to illustrate and enforce His teaching. It is a necessity to pray. It is exacting and binding for men always to be in prayer. Courage, endurance, and perseverance are demanded that men may never faint in prayer. "And shall not God avenge his own elect, which cry day and night unto him ... (Luke 18:7a)?

This is His strong and indignant questioning and affirmation. Men must pray according to Christ's teaching. They must not get tired nor grow weary in praying. God's character is the assured surety that much will come of the persistent praying of true men.

Doubtless the praying of our Lord had much to do with the revelation made to Peter and the confession he made to Christ, "Thou art the Christ, the Son of the living God." Prayer mightily affects and molds the circle of our associates. Christ made disciples and kept them disciples by praying. His twelve disciples were much impressed by His praying. Never man prayed like this man. How different His praying from the cold, proud, self-righteous praying which they heard and saw on the streets, in the synagogue, and in the temple.

17
Our Lord's Model Prayer

What satisfaction must it be to learn from God Himself with what words and in what manner, He would have us pray to Him so as not to pray in vain! We do not sufficiently consider the value of this prayer; the respect and attention which it requires; the preference to be given to it; its fulness and perfection; the frequent use we should make of it; and the spirit which we should bring with it. "Lord, teach us how to pray." — Adam Clark

Jesus gives us the pattern prayer in what is commonly known as the Lord's Prayer.

In this model, perfect prayer He gives us a law form to be followed, and yet one to be filled in and enlarged as we may decide when we pray. The outlines and form are complete, yet it is but an outline, with many a blank, which our needs and convictions are to fill in.

Christ puts words on our lips, words which are to be uttered by holy lives. Words belong to the life of prayer. Wordless prayers are like human spirits; pure and high they may be, but too ethereal and impalpable for earthly conflicts and earthly needs and uses. We must have spirits clothed in flesh and blood, and our prayers must be likewise clothed in words to give them point and power, a local habitation, and a name.

This lesson of the Lord's Prayer, drawn forth by the request of the disciples, "Lord, teach us to pray," has something in form and verbiage like the prayer sections of the Sermon on the Mount. It is the same great lesson of praying to "Our Father which art in heaven," and is one of insistent importunity. No prayer lesson would be complete without it. It belongs to the first and last lessons in prayer. God's fatherhood gives shape, value, and confidence to all our praying.

He teaches us that to hallow God's name is the first and the greatest of prayers. A desire for the glorious coming and the glorious establishment of God's glorious kingdom follows in value and in sequence the hallowing of God's name. He who really hallows God's name will hail the coming of the kingdom of God, and will labor and pray to bring that kingdom to pass and to establish it. Christ's pupils in the school of prayer are to be taught diligently to hallow God's name, to work for God's kingdom, and to do God's will perfectly, completely, and gladly, as it is done in heaven.

Prayer engages the highest interest and secures the highest glory of God. God's name, God's kingdom, and God's will are all in it. Without prayer His name is profaned, His kingdom fails, and His will is decried and opposed. God's will can be done on earth as it is done in heaven. God's will done on earth makes earth like heaven. Importunate praying is the mighty energy which establishes God's will on earth as it is established in heaven.

He is still teaching us that prayer sanctifies and makes

hopeful and sweet our daily toil for daily bread. Forgiveness of sins is to be sought by prayer, and the great prayer plea we are to make for forgiveness is that we have forgiven all those who have sinned against us. It involves love for our enemies so far as to pray for them, to bless them and not curse them, and to pardon their offenses against us whatever those offenses may be.

We are to pray, "lead us not into temptation," that is, that while we thus pray, the tempter and the temptation are to be watched against, resisted, and prayed against.

All these things He had laid down in this law of prayer, but many a simple lesson of comment, expansion, and expression He adds to His statute law.

In this prayer He teaches His disciples, so familiar to thousands in this day who learned it at their mother's knees in childhood, the words are so childlike that children find their instruction, edification, and comfort in them as they kneel and pray. The most glowing mystic and the most careful thinker finds each his own language in these simple words of prayer. Beautiful and revered as these words are, they are our words for solace, help, and learning.

He led the way in prayer that we might follow His footsteps. Matchless leader in matchless praying! Lord, teach us to pray as Thou didst Thyself pray!

How marked the contrast between the sacerdotal prayer and this Lord's Prayer, this copy for praying He gave to His disciples as the first elements of prayer. How simple and childlike! No one has ever approached in composition a prayer so simple in its petitions and yet so comprehensive in all of its requests.

How these simple elements of prayer as given by our Lord commend themselves to us! This prayer is for us as well as for those to whom it was first given. It is for the child in the A B C of prayer, and it is for the graduate of the highest institutions of learning. It is a personal prayer, reaching to all our needs and covering all our sins. It is the highest form of prayer for others. As the scholar can never in all his after studies or learning dispense with his A B C, and as the alphabet gives form, color, and expression to all after learning, impregnating all and grounding all, so the learner in Christ can never dispense with the Lord's Prayer. But he may make it form the basis of his higher praying, this intercession for others in the sacerdotal prayer.

The Lord's Prayer is ours by our mother's knee and fits us in all the stages of a joyous Christian life. The sacerdotal prayer is ours also in the stages and office of our royal priesthood as intercessors before God. Here we have oneness with God, deep spiritual unity, and unswerving loyalty to God, living and praying to glorify God.

Excerpts from

The Possibilities of Prayer

The Ministry of Prayer
Prayer—Its Wide Range
Answered Prayer
Prayer and Divine Providence

18
The Ministry of Prayer

"Prayer should be the breath of our breathing,
the thought of our thinking, the soul of our feeling,
and the life of our living, the sound of our hearing,
the growth of our growing." Prayer in its
magnitude is length without end, width without
bounds, height without top, and depth without
bottom. Illimitable in its breadth, exhaustless in
height, fathomless in depths and infinite in
extension. — Homer W. Hodge

The ministry of prayer has been the peculiar distinction of all of God's saints.

This has been the secret of their power. The energy and the soul of their work has been the closet. The need of help outside of man being so great, man's natural inability to always judge kindly, justly, and truly, and to act the golden rule, so prayer is enjoined by Christ to enable man to act in all these things according to the divine will. By prayer, the ability is secured to feel the law of love, to speak according to the law of love, and to do everything in harmony with the law of love.

God can help us. God is a Father. We need God's

good things to help us to "do justly, to love mercy, and to walk humbly before God." We need divine aid to act brotherly, wisely, and nobly, and to judge truly, and charitably. God's help to do all these things in God's way is secured by prayer. "Ask, and it shall be given you; seek, and ye shall find; knock, and it shall be opened unto you" (Matt. 7:7).

In the marvelous output of Christian graces and duties, the result of giving ourselves wholly to God, recorded in the twelfth chapter of Romans, we have the words, "continuing instant in prayer," preceded by "Rejoicing in hope; patient in tribulation," followed by, "Distributing to the necessity of saints; given to hospitality." Paul thus writes as if these rich and rare graces and unselfish duties, so sweet, bright, generous, and unselfish, had for their center and source the ability to pray.

This is the same word which is used of the prayer of the disciples which ushered in Pentecost with all of its rich and glorious blessings of the Holy Spirit. In Colossians, Paul presses the word into the service of prayer again, "Continue in prayer, and watch in the same with thanksgiving" (4:2). The word in its background and root means strong, the ability to stay, and persevere steadfast, to hold fast and firm, to give constant attention to.

In Acts, chapter six, it is translated, "give ourselves continually to prayer." There is in it constancy, courage, unfainting perseverance. It means giving such marked attention to and such deep concern to a thing as will make it conspicuous and controlling.

This is an advance in demand on "continue." Prayer is to be incessant, without intermission, assiduously, no check in desire, in spirit or in act, the spirit and the life always in the attitude of prayer. The knees may not always be bended, the lips may not always be vocal with words of prayer, but the spirit is always in the act and intercourse of prayer.

There ought to be no adjustment of life or spirit for closet hours. The closet spirit should sweetly rule and adjust all times and occasions. Our activities and work should be performed in the same spirit which makes our devotion and which makes our closet time sacred. "Without intermission, incessantly, assiduously," describes an opulence, and energy, and unabated and ceaseless strength and fullness of effort; like the full and exhaustless and spontaneous flow of an artesian stream. Touch the man of God who thus understands prayer, at any point, at any time, and a full current of prayer is seen flowing from him.

But all these untold benefits, of which the Holy Spirit is made to us the conveyor, go back in their disposition and results to prayer. Not on a little process and a mere performance of prayer is the coming of the Holy Spirit and of His great grace conditioned, but on prayer set on fire, by an unquenchable desire, with such a sense of need as cannot be denied, with a fixed determination which will not let go, and which will never faint till it wins the greatest good and gets the best and last blessing God has in store for us.

The first Christ, Jesus, our great High Priest, forever blessed and adored be His name, was a gracious comforter, a faithful guide, a gifted teacher, a fearless advocate, a devoted friend, and an all powerful intercessor. The other, "another Comforter," the Holy Spirit, comes into all these blessed relations to fellowship, authority, and aid with all the tenderness, sweetness, fullness and efficiency of the first Christ.

Was the first Christ the Christ of prayer? Did He offer prayers and supplications with strong crying and tears unto God? Did He seek the silence, the solitude and the darkness that He might pray unheard and unwitnessed save by heaven, in His wrestling agony for man with God? Does He ever live, enthroned above at the Father's right hand, there to pray for us?

Then how truly does the other Christ, the other Comforter, the Holy Spirit, represent Jesus Christ as the Christ of prayer! This other Christ, the Comforter, plants Himself not in the waste of the mountain nor far into the night, but in the chill and the night of the human heart, to rouse it to the struggle, and to teach it the need and form of prayer. How the divine Comforter, the spirit of truth, puts into the human heart the burden of earth's almighty need, and makes the human lips give voice to its mute and unutterable groanings!

What a mighty Christ of prayer is the Holy Spirit! How He quenches every flame in the heart but the flame of heavenly desire! How He quiets, like a weaned child, all the self-will, until in will, in brain, and in heart, and by mouth, we pray only as He prays, making "intercession for the saints according to the will of God" (Rom. 8:27).

19

Prayer — Its
Wide Range

Nothing so pleases God in connection with our prayer as our praise, . . . and nothing so blesses the man who prays as the praise which he offers. I got a great blessing once in China in this connection. I had received bad and sad news from home, and deep shadows had covered my soul. I prayed, but the darkness did not vanish. I summoned myself to endure, but the darkness only deepened. Just then I went to an inland station and saw on the wall of the mission home these words: "Try Thanksgiving." I did, and in a moment every shadow was gone, not to return. Yes, the Psalmist was right, "It is a good thing to give thanks unto the Lord." — Henry W. Frost

The possibilities of prayer are gauged by faith in God's ability to do. Faith is the one prime condition by which God works. Faith is the one prime condition by which man prays. Faith draws on God to its full extent. Faith gives character to prayer. A feeble faith has always brought forth feeble praying. Vigorous faith creates vigorous praying. At the close of a parable, "And he spake a parable unto them to this end, that men ought always to pray, and not to faint" (Luke 18:1), in which He stressed the necessity of vigorous praying, Christ asks this pointed question, "when the Son of man cometh, shall he find faith on the earth" (Luke 18:8)?

In the case of the lunatic child which the father brought first to the disciples, who could not cure him, and then to the Lord Jesus Christ, the father cried out with all the pathos of a declining faith and of a great sorrow, "if thou canst do anything, have compassion on us, and help us" (Mark 9:22) And Jesus said unto him, "If thou canst believe, all things are possible to him that believeth" (Mark 9:23). The healing turned on the faith in the ability of Christ to heal the boy. The ability to do was in Christ essentially and eternally, but the doing of the thing turned on the ability of the faith. Great faith enables Christ to do great things.

We need a quickening faith in God's power. We have hedged God in till we have little faith in His power. We have conditioned the exercise of His power till we have a little God, and a little faith in a little God.

The only condition which restrains God's power and which disables Him to act is unfaith. He is not limited in action nor restrained by the conditions which limit men.

The conditions of time, place, nearness, ability, and all others which could possibly be named, upon which the actions of men hinge, have no bearing on God. If men will look to God and cry to Him with true prayer, He will hear and can deliver, no matter how dire soever may be the state, how remediless their conditions may be.

Strange how God has to school His people in His ability to do! He made a promise to Abraham and Sarah that Isaac would be born. Abraham was then nearly 100 years old, and Sarah was barren by natural defect, and had passed into a barren, wombless age. She laughed at the thought of having a child as preposterous. God asked, "Why did Sarah laugh? Is anything too hard for the Lord?" And God fulfilled His promise to these old people to the letter.

Moses because of his inability to talk well, hesitated to undertake God's purpose to liberate Israel from Egyptian bondage. God checks him at once by an inquiry:

And Moses said unto the Lord, O my Lord, I am not eloquent, neither heretofore, nor since thou hast spoken unto thy servant: but I am slow of speech, and of a slow tongue.

And the Lord said unto him, Who hath made man's mouth? or who maketh the dumb, or deaf, or the seeing, or the blind? Have not I the Lord?

Now therefore go, and I will be with thy mouth, and teach thee what thou shalt say (Exod. 4:10-12).

When God said He would feed the children of Israel a whole month with meat, Moses questioned His ability to do it. The Lord said unto Moses, "Is the Lord's hand waxed short? thou shalt see now whether my word shall come to pass unto thee or not" (Num. 11:23).

Nothing is too hard for the Lord to do. As Paul declared, He "is able to do exceeding abundantly above all that we can ask or think." Prayer has to do with God, with His ability to do. The possibility of prayer is the measure of God's ability to do.

The "all things," the "all things whatsoever," and the "anything" are all covered by the ability of God. The urgent entreaty reads, "Ask whatsoever ye will," because God is able to do anything and all things that my desires may crave and that He has promised. In God's ability to do, He goes far beyond man's ability to ask. Human thoughts, human words, human imaginations, human desires, and human needs cannot in any way measure God's ability to do.

Prayer in its legitimate possibilities goes out on God Himself. Prayer goes out with faith not only in the promise of God but faith in God Himself and in God's ability to do. Prayer goes out not on the promise merely but "obtains promises" and creates promises.

Elijah had the promise that God would send the rain, but no promise that He would send the fire. But by faith and prayer he obtained the fire, as well as the rain, but the fire came first.

Daniel had no specific promise that God would make known to him the dream of the king, but he and his associates joined in united prayer, and God revealed to Daniel the king's dream and the interpretation, and their lives were spared thereby.

Hezekiah had no promise that God would cure him of his desperate sickness which threatened his life. On the contrary the word of the Lord came to him by the mouth of the prophet, that he should die. However, he prayed against this decree of almighty God with faith, and he succeeded in obtaining a reversal of God's word and lived.

God makes it marvelous when He says by the mouth of His prophet: "Thus saith the Lord, the Holy One of Israel, and his Maker, Ask me of things to come concerning my sons, and concerning the work of my hands command ye me" (Isa. 45:11). And in this strong promise in which He commits Himself into the hands of His praying people, He appeals in it to His great creative power: "I have made the earth, and created man upon it:

I, even my hands, have stretched out the heavens, and all their host have I commanded" (Isa. 45:12).

The majesty and power of God in making man and man's world, and constantly upholding all things, are ever kept before us as the basis of our faith in God, and as an assurance and urgency to prayer. Then God calls us away from what He Himself has done, and turns our minds to Himself personally. The infinite glory and power of His person are set before our contemplation: "Remember ye not the former things, neither consider the things of old" (Isa. 43:18). He declares that He will do a "new thing," that He does not have to repeat Himself, that all He has done neither limits His doing nor the manner of His doing, and that if we have prayer and faith, He will so answer our prayers and so work for us that His former work shall not be remembered nor come into mind. If men would pray as they ought to pray, the marvels of the past would be more than reproduced. The gospel would advance with a facility and power it has never known. Doors would be thrown open to the gospel, and the Word of God would have a conquering force rarely if ever known before.

If Christians prayed as Christians ought, with strong commanding faith, with earnestness and sincerity, men, God-called men, God-empowered men everywhere, would be all burning to go and spread the gospel worldwide. The Word of the Lord would run and be glorified as never known heretofore. The God-influenced men, the God-inspired men, the God-commissioned men, would go and kindle the flame of sacred fire for Christ, salvation, and heaven, everywhere in all nations, and soon all men would hear the glad tidings of salvation and have an opportunity to receive Jesus Christ as their personal Savior. Let us read another one of those large illimitable

statements in God's Word, which are a direct challenge
to prayer and faith:

> He that spared not his own Son, but delivered him up
> for us all, how shall he not with him freely give us all
> things (Rom. 8:32)?

What a basis have we here for prayer and faith, illimitable, measureless in breadth, in depth, and in height!
The promise to give us all things is backed up by the
calling to our remembrance of the fact that God freely
gave His only begotten Son for our redemption. His giving His Son is the assurance and guarantee that He will
freely give all things to him who believes and prays.

What confidence have we in this Divine statement for
inspired asking! What holy boldness we have here for
the largest asking! No commonplace tameness should
restrain our largest asking. Large, larger, and largest asking magnifies grace and adds to God's glory. Feeble asking impoverishes the asker, restrains God's purposes for
the greatest good, and obscures His glory.

How enthroned, magnificent, and royal the intercession of our Lord Jesus Christ at His Father's right hand
in heaven! The benefits of His intercession flow to us
through our intercessions. Our intercession ought to catch
by contagion and by necessity the inspiration and large-
ness of Christ's great work at His Father's right hand.
His business and His life are to pray. Our business and
our lives ought to be to pray, and to pray without ceasing.

Failure in our intercession affects the fruits of His
intercession. Lazy, heartless, feeble, and indifferent praying by us mars and hinders the effects of Christ's praying.

20
Answered Prayer

In his "Soldier's Pocket Book," Lord Wolseley says if a young officer wishes to get on, he must volunteer for the most hazardous duties and take every possible chance of risking his life. It was a spirit and courage like that which was shown in the service of God by a good soldier of Jesus Christ named John McKenzie who died a few years ago. One evening when he was a lad and eager for work in the Foreign Mission field he knelt down at the foot of a tree in the Ladies' Walk on the banks of the Lossie at Elgin and offered up this prayer: "O Lord send me to the darkest spot on earth." And God heard him and sent him to South Africa where he laboured many years first under the London Missionary Society and then under the British Government as the first Resident Commissioner among the natives of Bechuanaland. — J. O. Struthers

It is answered prayer which brings praying out of the realm of dry, dead things, and makes praying a thing of life and power. It is the answer to prayer which brings things to pass, changes the natural trend of things, and orders all things according to the will of God. It is the answer to prayer which takes praying out of the regions of fanaticism and saves it from being utopian, or from being merely fanciful. It is the answer to prayer which makes praying a power for God and for man and makes praying real and divine. Unanswered prayers are training schools for unbelief, an imposition and a nuisance, an impertinence to God and to man.

Answers to prayer are the only surety that we have prayed aright. What marvelous power there is in prayer! What untold miracles it works in this world! What untold benefits to men does it secure to those who pray! Why is it that the average prayer by the million goes a begging for an answer?

The millions of unanswered prayers are not to be solved by the mystery of God's will. We are not the sport of His sovereign power. He is not playing at "make believe" in His marvelous promises to answer prayer. The whole explanation is found in our wrong praying. "We ask and receive not because we ask amiss." If all unanswered prayers were dumped into the ocean, they would come very near filling it. Child of God, can you pray? Are your prayers answered? If not, why not? Answered prayer is the proof of your real praying.

The efficacy of prayer from a Bible standpoint lies solely in the answer to prayer. The benefit of prayer has been well and popularly maximized by the saying, "It moves the arm which moves the universe." To get unquestioned answers to prayer is not only important as to the satisfying of our desires, but is the evidence of our abiding in Christ. It becomes more important still. The mere act of praying is no test of our relation to God. The act of praying may be a real dead performance. It may be the routine of habit. But to pray and receive clear answers, not once or twice, but daily, this is the sure test, and is the gracious point of our vital connection with Jesus Christ.

Read our Lord's words in this connection:

> If ye abide in me, and my words abide in you, ye shall ask what ye will, and it shall be done unto you" (John 15:7).

To God and to man, the answer to prayer is the all-important part of our praying. The answer to prayer, direct and unmistakable, is the evidence of God's being. It proves that God lives, that there is a God, an intelligent being, who is interested in His creatures, and who listens to them when they approach Him in prayer. There is no proof so clear and demonstrative that God exists than prayer and its answer. This was Elijah's plea: "Hear me, O Lord, hear me, that this people may know that thou art the Lord God" (I Kings 18:37a).

The answer to prayer is the part of prayer which glorifies God. Unanswered prayers are dumb oracles which leave the praying ones in darkness, doubt, and bewilderment and which carry no conviction to the unbeliever. It is not the act or the attitude of praying which gives efficacy to prayer. It is not abject prostration of the body before God, the vehement or quiet utterance to God, the exquisite beauty and poetry of the diction of our prayers, which do the deed. It is not the marvelous array of argument and eloquence in praying which makes prayer effectual. Not one or all of these are the things which glorify God. It is the answer which brings glory to His name.

Elijah might have prayed on Carmel's heights till this good day with all the fire and energy of his soul, and if no answer had been given, no glory would have come to God. Peter might have shut himself up with Dorcas's dead body till he himself died on his knees, and if no answer had come, no glory to God nor good to man would have followed, but only doubt, blight, and dismay.

Answer to prayer is the convincing proof of our right relations to God. Jesus said at the grave of Lazarus:

Father, I thank thee that thou hast heard me.

And I knew that thou hearest me always: but because of the people which stand by I said it, that they may believe that thou hast sent me (John 11:41a, 42).

The answer of His prayer was the proof of His mission from God, as the answer to Elijah's prayer was made to the woman whose son he raised to life. She said, "Now by this I know that thou art a man of God." He is highest in the favor of God who has the readiest access and the greatest number of answers to prayer from almighty God.

Prayer ascends to God by an invariable law, even by more than law, by the will, the promise and the presence of a personal God. The answer comes back to earth by all the promise, the truth, the power and the love of God.

Not to be concerned about the answer to prayer is not to pray. What a world of waste there is in praying. What myriads of prayers have been offered for which no answer is returned, no answer longed for, and no answer is expected! We have been nurturing a false faith and hiding the shame of our loss and inability to pray, by the false, comforting plea that God does not answer directly or objectively, but indirectly and subjectively. We have persuaded ourselves that by some kind of hocus-pocus of which we are wholly unconscious in its process and its results, we have been made better. Conscious that God has not answered us directly, we have solaced ourselves with the delusive unction that God has in some impalpable way, and with unknown results, given us something better. Or we have comforted and nurtured our spiritual sloth by saying that it is not God's will to give it to us. Faith teaches God's praying ones that it is God's will to answer prayer. God answers all prayers and every prayer of His true children who truly pray.

> Prayer makes the darkened cloud withdraw,
> Prayer climbs the ladder Jacob saw;
> Gives exercise to faith and love,
> Brings every blessing from above.

The emphasis in the Scriptures is always given to the answer to prayer. All things from God are given in answer to prayer. God Himself, His presence, His gifts, and His grace, one and all, are secured by prayer. The medium by which God communicates with men is prayer. The most real thing in prayer, its very essential end, is the answer it secures. The mere repetition of words in prayer, the counting of beads, the multiplying mere words of prayer, as works of supererogation, as if there was virtue in the number of prayers to avail, is a vain delusion, an empty thing, a useless service. Prayer looks directly to securing an answer. This is its design. It has no other end in view.

Communion with God of course is in prayer. There is sweet fellowship there with our God through His Holy Spirit. Enjoyment of God there is in praying, sweet, rich, and strong. The graces of the Spirit in the inner soul are nurtured by prayer, kept alive and promoted in their growth by this spiritual exercise. But not one nor all of these benefits of prayer have in them the essential end of prayer. The divinely-appointed channel through which all good and all grace flows to our souls and bodies is prayer.

> Prayer is appointed to convey
> The blessings God designs to give.

Prayer is divinely ordained as the means by which all temporal and spiritual good are gained to us. Prayer is not an end in itself. It is not something done to be rested in, something we have done, about which we are to congratulate ourselves. It is a means to an end. It is something we do which brings us something in return, without which the praying is valueless. Prayer always aims at securing an answer.

We are rich and strong, good and holy, beneficent and benignant, by answered prayer. It is not the mere performance, the attitude, nor the words of prayer which bring benefit to us, but it is the answer sent direct from heaven. Conscious, real answers to prayer bring real good to us. This is not praying merely for self, or simply for selfish ends. The selfish character cannot exist when the prayer conditions are fulfilled.

It is by these answered prayers that human nature is enriched. The answered prayer brings us into constant and conscious communion with God, awakens and enlarges gratitude, and excites the melody and lofty inspiration of praise. Answered prayer is the mark of God in our praying. It is the exchange with heaven, and it establishes and realizes a relationship with the unseen. We give our prayers in exchange for the divine blessing. God accepts our prayers through the atoning blood and gives Himself, His presence, and His grace in return.

All holy affections are affected by answered prayers. By the answers to prayer all holy principles are matured, and faith, love, and hope have their enrichment by answered prayer. The answer is found in all true praying. The answer is in prayer strongly as an aim, a desire expressed, and its expectation and realization give importunity and realization to prayer. It is the fact of the answer which makes the prayer, and which enters into its very being. To seek no answer to prayer takes the desire, the aim, and the heart out of prayer. It makes praying a dead, stockish thing, fit only for dumb idols. It is the answer which brings praying into Bible regions, and makes it a desire realized, a pursuit, an interest, that clothes it with flesh and blood, and makes it a prayer, throbbing with all the true life of prayer, affluent with all the paternal relations of giving and receiving, of asking and answering.

God holds all good in His own hands. That good comes to us through our Lord Jesus Christ because of His all-atoning merits, by asking it in His name. The only and the sole command in which all the others of its class belong, is "Ask, seek, knock." And the one and sole promise is its counterpart, its necessary equivalent and results: "It shall be given — ye shall find — it shall be opened unto you."

God is so much involved in prayer and its hearing and answering that all of His attributes and His whole being are centered in that great fact. It distinguishes Him as peculiarly beneficent, wonderfully good, and powerfully attractive in His nature. "O thou that hearest prayer! To thee shall all flesh come."

> Faithful, O Lord, Thy mercies are
>   A rock that cannot move;
> A thousand promises declare
>   Thy constancy of love.

Not only does the Word of God stand surety for the answer to prayer, but all the attributes of God conspire to the same end. God's veracity is at stake in the engagements to answer prayer. His wisdom, His truthfulness, and His goodness are involved. God's infinite and inflexible rectitude is pledged to the great end of answering the prayers of those who call upon Him in time of need. Justice and mercy blend into oneness to secure the answer to prayer. It is significant that the very justice of God comes into play and stands hard by God's faithfulness in the strong promise God makes of the pardon of sins and of cleansing from sin's pollutions:

> If we confess our sins, he is faithful and just to forgive us our sins and, to cleanse us from all unrighteousness (I John 1:9).

God's kingly relation to man, with all of its authority, unites with the fatherly relation and with all of its tenderness to secure the answer to prayer.

Our Lord Jesus Christ is most fully committed to the answer of prayer. "And whatsoever ye shall ask in my name, that will I do, that the Father may be glorified in the Son" (John 14:13). How well assured the answer to prayer is when that answer is to glorify God the Father! And how eager Jesus Christ is to glorify His Father in heaven! So eager is He to answer prayer which always and everywhere brings glory to the Father that no prayer offered in His name is denied or overlooked by Him. Says our Lord Jesus Christ again, giving fresh assurance to our faith, "If ye shall ask any thing in my name, I will do it" (John 14:14). So says He once more, ". . . ask what ye will, and it shall be done unto you" (John 15:7b).

> Come, my soul, thy suit prepare,
> Jesus loves to answer prayer;
> He Himself has bid thee pray,
> Therefore will not say thee nay.

> Constrained at the darkest hour to confess
> humbly that without God's help I was helpless, I
> vowed a vow in the forest solitude that I would

confess His aid before men. A silence as a death
was around me; it was midnight, I was weakened
by illness, prostrated with fatigue and worn with
anxiety for my white and black companions, whose
fate was a mystery. In this physical and mental
distress I besought God to give me back my
people. Nine hours later we were exulting with
rapturous joy. In full view of all was the crimson
flag with the crescent and beneath its waving folds
was the long-lost rear columns. — Henry M. Stanley

God has committed Himself to us by His Word
in our praying. The Word of God is the basis and the
inspiration and the heart of prayer. Jesus Christ stands
as the illustration of God's Word, its illimitable good in
promise as well as in realization. God takes nothing by
halves. He gives nothing by halves. We can have the
whole of Him when He has the whole of us. His words
of promise are so far-reaching and so all-comprehending
that they seem to have deadened our comprehension and
have paralyzed our praying. This appears when we consider those large words, when He almost exhausts human
language in promises, as in "whatever," "anything," and
in the all-inclusive "whatsoever," and "all things." These
oft-repeated promises, so very great, seem to daze us,
and instead of allowing them to move us to asking, testing, and receiving, we turn away full of wonder, but
empty handed and with empty hearts.

We quote another passage from our Lord's teaching
about prayer. By the most solemn verification, He declares as follows:

And in that day ye shall ask me nothing. Verily, verily,
I say unto you, Whatsoever ye shall ask the Father in
my name, he will give it to you.

Hitherto have ye asked nothing in my name: ask, and ye shall receive, that your joy may be full (John 16:23, 24).

Twice in this passage He declares the answer, and pledging His Father, "he will give it to you," and declaring with impressive and most suggestive iteration, "ask, and ye shall receive." So strong and so often did Jesus declare and repeat the answer as an inducement to pray, and as an inevitable result of prayer, the apostles held it as so fully and invincibly established that prayer would be answered; they held it to be their main duty to urge and command men to pray. So firmly were they established as to the truth of the law of prayer as laid down by our Lord, that they were led to affirm that the answer to prayer was involved in and necessarily bound up with all right praying. God the Father and Jesus Christ, His Son, are both strongly committed by all the truth of their word and by the fidelity of their character, to answer prayer.

Not only do these and all the promises pledge almighty God to answer prayer, but they assure us that the answer will be specific, and that the very thing for which we pray will be given.

Our Lord's invariable teaching was that we receive that for which we ask, and obtain that for which we seek, and have that door opened at which we knock. This is according to our heavenly Father's direction to us, and His giving to us for our asking. He will not disappoint us by not answering, neither will He deny us by giving us some other thing for which we have not asked, or by letting us find some other thing for which we have not sought, or by opening to us the wrong door, at which we were not knocking. If we ask bread, He will give us bread. If we ask an egg, He will give us an egg. If we ask a fish, He will give us a fish. Not something like bread, but bread itself will be given unto us. Not something like a fish, but a fish will be given. Not evil will be given us in answer to prayer, but good.

Earthly parents, though evil in nature, give for the asking, and answer to the crying of their children. The encouragement to prayer is transferred from our earthly father to our heavenly Father, from the evil to the good, to the supremely good; from the weak to the omnipotent, our heavenly Father, centering in Himself all the highest conceptions of fatherhood, abler, readier, and much more than the best, and much more than the ablest earthly father. "How much more," who can tell? Much more than our earthly father will He supply all our needs, give us all good things, and enable us to meet every difficult duty and fulfill every law, though hard to flesh and blood, but made easy under the full supply of our Father's beneficent and exhaustless help.

Here we have in symbol and as initial more than an intimation of the necessity, not only of perseverance in prayer, but of the progressive stages of intentness and effort in the outlay of increasing spiritual force. Asking, seeking, and knocking. Here is an ascending scale from the mere words of asking, to a settled attitude of seeking, resulting in a determined, clamorous, and vigorous direct effort of praying.

Just as God has commanded us to pray always, to pray everywhere, and to pray in everything, so He will answer always, everywhere, and in everything.

God has plainly and with directness committed Himself to answer prayer. If we fulfill the conditions of prayer, the answer is bound to come. The laws of nature are not so invariable and so inexorable as the promised answer to pray. The ordinances of nature might fail, but the ordinances of grace can never fail. There are no limitations, no adverse conditions, no weakness, no inability which can or will hinder the answer to prayer. God's doing for us when we pray has no limitations, is not hedged about by provisos in Himself or in the peculiar circumstances of any particular case. If we really pray, God masters and defies all things and is above all conditions.

God explicitly says, "Call unto me, and I will answer." There are no limitations, no hedges, no hindrances in the way of God fulfilling the promise. His word is at stake. His word is involved. God solemnly engages to answer prayer. Man is to look for the answer, be inspired by the expectation of the answer, and may with humble boldness demand the answer. God, who cannot lie, is bound to answer. He has voluntarily placed Himself under obligation to answer the prayer of him who truly prays.

> To God your every want
>   In instant prayer display;
> Pray always; pray, and never faint;
>   Pray, without ceasing, pray.
>
> In fellowship, alone,
>   To God with faith draw near;
> Approach His courts, beseech His throne,
>   With all the power of prayer.

The prophets and the men of God of Old Testament times were unshaken in their faith in the absolute certainty of God fulfilling His promises to them. They rested in security on the word of God and had no doubt whatever either as to the fidelity of God in answering prayer or of His willingness or ability. So that their history is marked by repeated asking and receiving at the hands of God.

The same is true of the early church. They received without question the doctrine their Lord and Master had so often affirmed that the answer to prayer was sure. The certainty of the answer to prayer was as fixed as God's Word was true. The Holy Ghost dispensation was ushered in by the disciples carrying this faith into practice. When Jesus told them to "tarry at Jerusalem till they were endued with power from on high," they received it as a sure promise that if they obeyed the command they would certainly receive the divine power. So in prayer for ten days they tarried in the upper room, and the promise was fulfilled. The answer came just as Jesus said.

So when Peter and John were arrested for healing the man who sat at the beautiful gate of the temple, after being threatened by the rulers in Jerusalem, they were released. "And being let go, they went to their own company," they went to those with whom they were in affinity, those of like minds, and not to men of the world. Still believing in prayer and its efficacy, they gave themselves to prayer, the prayer itself being recorded in Acts 4:31. They recited some things to the Lord, "And when they had prayed, the place was shaken where they were assembled together; and they were filled with the Holy Ghost, and they spake the word of God with boldness."

Here they were refilled for this special occasion with the Holy Ghost. The answer to prayer responded to their faith and prayer. The fullness of the Spirit always brings boldness. The cure for fear in the face of threatenings of the enemies of the Lord is being filled with the Spirit. This gives power to speak the Word of the Lord with boldness. This gives courage and drives away fear.

A young man had been called to the foreign field. He had not been in the habit of preaching, but he knew one thing, how to prevail with God; and going one day to a friend he said: "I don't see how God can use me on the field. I have no special talent." His friend said: "My brother, God wants men on the field who can pray. There are too many preachers now and too few pray-ers." He went. In his own room in the early dawn a voice was heard weeping and pleading for souls. All through the day, the shut door and the hush that prevailed made you feel like walking softly, for a soul was wrestling with God.

Yet to this home, hungry souls would flock, drawn by some irresistible power.

Ah, the mystery was unlocked. In the secret chamber lost souls were pleaded for and claimed. The Holy Ghost knew just where they were and sent them along.—J. Hudson Taylor

We put it to the front. We unfold it on a banner never to be lowered or folded, that God does hear and answer prayer. God has always heard and answered prayer. God will forever hear and answer prayer. He is the same yesterday, today, and forever, ever blessed, ever to be adorned. Amen. He changes not. As He has always answered prayer, so will He ever continue to do so.

To answer prayer is God's universal rule. It is His unchangeable and irrepealable law to answer prayer. It is His invariable, specific, and inviolate promise to answer prayer. The few denials to prayer in the Scriptures are the exceptions to the general rule, suggestive and startling by their fewness, exception, and emphasis.

The possibilities of prayer, then, lie in the great truth, illimitable in its broadness, fathomless in its depths, exhaustless in its fullness, that God answers every prayer from every true soul who truly prays.

God's Word does not say, "Call unto me, and you will thereby be trained into the happy art of knowing how to be denied. Ask, and you will learn sweet patience by getting nothing." Far from it. But it is definite, clear, and positive: "Ask, and it shall be given unto you."

We have this case among many in the Old Testament:

> And Jabez called on the God of Israel, saying, Oh that thou wouldst bless me indeed, and enlarge my coast, and that thine hand might be with me, and that thou wouldst keep me from evil, that it may not grieve me (I Chron. 4:10a).

And God readily granted him the things which he had requested.

Hannah, distressed in soul because she was childless, and desiring a man child, repaired to the house of prayer and prayed, and this is the record she makes of the direct answer she received: "For this child I prayed; and the Lord hath given me my petition which I asked of him" (I Sam. 1:27).

God's promises and purposes go direct to the fact of giving for the asking. The answer to our prayers is the motive constantly presented in the Scriptures to encourage us to pray and to quicken us in this spiritual exercise. Take such strong, clear passages as these:

> Call unto me, and I will answer thee.

> He shall call unto me, and I will answer.

> Ask, and it shall be given you. Seek, and ye shall find. Knock, and it shall be opened unto you.

This is Jesus Christ's law of prayer. He does not say, "Ask, and something shall be given you." Nor does He say, "Ask, and you will be trained into piety." But it is that when you ask, the very thing asked for will be given. Jesus does not say, "Knock, and some door will be opened." But the very door at which you are knocking will be opened. To make this doubly sure, Jesus Christ duplicates and reiterates the promise of the answer: "For every one that asketh receiveth; and he that seeketh findeth; and to him that knocketh it shall be opened" (Matt. 7:8).

Answered prayer is the spring of love, and is the direct encouragement to pray. "I love the Lord, because he hath heard my voice and my supplications. Because he hath inclined his ear unto me, therefore will I call upon him as long as I live" (Ps. 116:1, 2).

The certainty of the Father's giving is assured by the Father's relation and by the ability and goodness of the Father. Earthly parents, frail, infirm, and limited in goodness and ability, give when the child asks and seeks. The parental heart responds most readily to the cry for bread. The hunger of the child touches and wins the father heart. So God, our heavenly Father, is as easily and strongly moved by our prayers as the earthly parent. "If ye then, being evil, know how to give good gifts unto your children, how much more shall your Father which is in heaven give good things to them that ask him" (Matt. 7:11)? "Much more," just as much more does God's goodness, tenderness, and ability exceed that of man's.

Just as the asking is specific, so also is the answer specific. The child does not ask for one thing and get another. He does not cry for bread, and get a stone. He does not ask for an egg, and receive a scorpion. He does not ask for a fish, and get a serpent. Christ demands specific asking. He responds to specific praying by specific giving.

To give the very thing prayed for, and not something else, is fundamental to Christ's law of praying. No prayer for the cure of blind eyes did He ever answer by curing deaf ears. The very thing prayed for is the very thing which He gives. The exceptions to this are confirmatory of this great law of prayer. He who asks for bread gets bread, and not a stone. If he asks for a fish, he receives a fish, and not a serpent. No cry is so pleading and so powerful as the child's cry for bread. The cravings of hunger, the appetite felt, and the need realized, all create and propel the crying of the child. Our prayers must be as earnest, as needy, and as hungry as the hungry child's cry for bread. Simple, artless, and direct and specific must be our praying, according to Christ's law of prayer and His teaching of God's Fatherhood.

The illustration and enforcement of the law of prayer are found in the specific answers given to prayer. Gethsemane is the only seeming exception. The prayer of Jesus Christ in that awful hour of darkness and hell was conditioned on these words, "if it be possible, let this cup pass from me." But beyond these utterances of our Lord was the soul and life prayer of the willing, suffering divine victim, "nevertheless not as I will, but as thou wilt." The prayer was answered, the angel came, strength was imparted, and the meek sufferer in silence drank the bitter cup.

Two cases of unanswered prayer are recorded in the Scriptures in addition to the Gethsemane prayer of our Lord. The first was that of David for the life of his baby child, but for good reasons to almighty God the request was not granted. The second was that of Paul for the removal of the thorn in the flesh, which was denied. But we are constrained to believe these must have been notable as exceptions to God's rule, as illustrated in the history of prophet, priest, apostle and saint, as recorded in the divine Word. There must have been unrevealed reasons which moved God to veer from His settled and fixed rule to answer prayer by giving the specific thing prayed for.

Our Lord did not hold the Syrophoenician woman in the school of unanswered prayer in order to test and mature her faith, neither did He answer her prayer by healing or saving her husband. She asked for the healing of her daughter, and Christ healed the daughter. She received the very thing for which she asked the Lord Jesus Christ. It was in the school of answered prayer our Lord disciplined and perfected her faith, and it was by giving her a specific answer to her prayer. Her prayer centered on her daughter. She prayed for the one thing, the healing of her child. And the answer of our Lord centered likewise on the daughter.

We tread altogether too gingerly upon the great and precious promises of God, and too often we ignore them wholly. The promise is the ground on which faith stands in asking of God. This is the one basis of prayer. We limit God's ability. We measure God's ability and willingness to answer by prayer by the standard of men. We limit the Holy One of Israel. How full of benefaction and remedy to suffering mankind are the promises as given us by James in his epistle, fifth chapter! How personal and mediate do they make God in prayer! They are a direct challenge to our faith. They are encouraging to large expectations in all the requests we make of God. Prayer affects God in a direct manner, and has its aim and end in affecting Him. Prayer takes hold of God, and induces Him to do large things for us, whether personal or relative, temporal or spiritual, earthly or heavenly.

The great gap between Bible promises to prayer and the income from praying is almost unspeakably great, so much so that it is a prolific source of infidelity. It breeds unbelief in prayer as a great moral force, and begets doubt really as to the efficacy of prayer. Christianity needs today, above all things else, men and women who can in prayer put God to the test and who can prove His promises. When this happy day for the world begins, it will be earth's brightest day and will be heaven's dawning day on earth. These are the sort of men and women needed in this modern day in the church. It is not educated men who are needed for the times. It is not more money that is required. It is not more machinery, more organization, more ecclesiastical laws, but it is men and women who know how to pray, who can in prayer lay hold upon God and bring Him down to earth, and move Him to take hold of earth's affairs mightily and put life and power into the church and into all of its machinery.

The church and the world greatly need saints who can bridge this wide gap between the praying done and the small number of answers received. Saints are needed whose faith is bold enough and sufficiently far-reaching to put God to the test. The cry comes even now out of heaven to the people of the present-day church, as it sounded forth in the days of Malachi: "prove me now herewith, saith the Lord of hosts." God is waiting to be put to the test by His people in prayer. He delights in being put to the test on His promises. It is His highest pleasure to answer prayer to prove the reliability of His promises. Nothing worthy of God nor of great value to men will be accomplished till this is done.

Our gospel belongs to the miraculous. It was projected on the miraculous plane. It cannot be maintained but by the supernatural. Take the supernatural out of our holy religion, and its life and power are gone, and it degenerates into a mere mode of morals. The miraculous is divine power. Prayer has in it this same power. Prayer brings this divine power into the ranks of men and puts it to work. Prayer brings into the affairs of earth a supernatural element. Our gospel when truly presented is the power of God. Never was the church more in need of those who can and will test almighty God. Never did the church need more than now those who can raise up everywhere memorials of God's supernatural power, memorials of answers to prayer, memorials of promises fulfilled. These would do more to silence the enemy of souls, the foe of God, and the adversary of the church than any modern scheme or present-day plan for the success of the gospel. Such memorials reared by praying people would dumbfound God's foes, strengthen weak saints, and would fill strong saints with triumphant rapture.

The most prolific source of infidelity, and that which traduces and hinders praying, and that which obscures the being and glory of God most effectually, is unanswered prayer. Better not to pray at all than to go through a dead form, which secures no answer, brings no glory to God, and supplies no good to man. Nothing so indurates the heart and nothing so blinds us to the unseen and the eternal, as this kind of prayerless praying.

21

Prayer and Divine Providence

Again a poor soul is tempted to doubt the being of a God; arguments by way of reason and wisdom may convince him he may get a little light from them; but sometimes God will come into his soul with an immediate beam and scatter all his doubts, more than a thousand arguments can do; the way of wisdom thus of knowing there is a God, that unties the knot; but the other cuts it in pieces presently; so it is in all temptations else a man goes the way of wisdom and sanctified reason, and looks into his own heart and there sees the work of grace and argues from all God's dealings with him; yet all these satisfy not a man: but God comes with a light in his spirit and all his bolts and shackles are knocked off in a moment; here we see the way of Wisdom and the way of Revelation.—Thomas Goodwin

Prayer and the divine providence are closely related. They stand in close companionship. They cannot possibly be separated. So closely connected are they that to deny one is to abolish the other. Prayer supposes a providence, while providence is the result of and belongs to prayer. All answers to prayer are but the intervention of the providence of God in the affairs of men. Providence has to do specially with praying people. Prayer, providence, and the Holy Spirit are a trinity, which cooperate with each other and are in perfect harmony with one another. Prayer is but the request of man for God through the Holy Spirit to interfere in behalf of him who prays.

What is termed providence is the divine superintendence over earth and its affairs. It implies gracious provisions which almighty God makes for all His creatures, animate and inanimate, intelligent or otherwise. Once admit that God is the Creator and Preserver of all men, and concede that He is wise and intelligent, and logically we are driven to the conclusion that almighty God has a direct superintendence of those whom He has created and whom He preserves in being. In fact creation and preservation suppose a superintending providence. What is called divine providence is simply almighty God governing the world for its best interests and overseeing everything for the good of mankind.

Men talk about a "general providence" as separate from a "special providence." There is no general providence but what is made up of special providences. A general supervision on the part of God supposes a special and individual supervision of each person, yea, even every creature, animal, and all alike.

God is everywhere, watching, superintending, overseeing, governing everything in the highest interest of man and carrying forward His plans and executing His purposes in creation and redemption. He is not an absentee God. He did not make the world with all that is in it and turn it over to so-called natural laws and then retire into the secret places of the universe having no regard for it or for the working of His laws. His hand is on the throttle. The work is not beyond His control. Earth's inhabitants and its affairs are not running independent of almighty God.

Any and all providences are special providences, and prayer and this sort of providences work hand in hand. God's hand is in everything. None are beyond Him nor beneath His notice. Not that God orders everything that comes to pass. Man is still a free agent, but the wisdom of almighty God comes out when we remember that while man is free and the devil is abroad in the land, God can superintend and overrule earth's affairs for the good of man and for His glory, and cause even the wrath of man to praise Him.

Nothing occurs by accident under the superintendence of an all-wise and perfectly just God. Nothing happens by chance in God's moral or natural government. God is a God of order, a God of law, but none the less a superintendent in the interest of His intelligent and redeemed creatures. Nothing can take place without the knowledge of God.

> His all surrounding sight surveys
> Our rising and our rest;
> Our public walks, our private ways,
> The secrets of our breasts.

Jesus Christ sets this matter at rest when He says, "Are not two sparrows sold for a farthing? and one of them shall not fall on the ground without your Father. But the very hairs of your head are all numbered. Fear ye not therefore, ye are of more value than many sparrows" (Matt. 10:29-31).

God cannot be ruled out of the world. The doctrine of prayer brings Him directly into the world, and moves Him to a direct interference with all of this world's affairs.

To rule almighty God out of the providences of life is to strike a direct blow at prayer and its efficacy. Nothing takes place in the world without God's consent, yet not in a sense that He either approves everything or is responsible for all things which happen. God is not the author of sin.

The question is sometimes asked, "Is God in everything?" as if there are some things which are outside of the government of God, beyond His attention, with which He is not concerned. If God is not in everything, what is the Christian doing praying according to Paul's directions to the Philippians?

> Be careful for nothing; but in every thing by prayer and supplication with thanksgiving let your requests be made known unto God (Phil. 4:6).

Are we to pray for some things and about things with which God has nothing to do? According to the doctrine that God is not in everything, then we are outside the realm of God when "in everything we make our requests unto God."

Then what will we do with that large promise so comforting to all of God's saints in all ages and in all climes, a promise which belongs to prayer and which is embraced in a special providence: "And we know that all things work together for good to them that love God" (Rom. 8:28a)?

If God is not in everything, then what are the things we are to expect from the "all things" which "work together for good to them that love God"? And if God is not in everything in His providence what are the things which are to be left out of our praying? We can lay it down as a proposition, borne out by Scripture, which has a sure foundation, that nothing ever comes into the life of God's saints without His consent. God is always there when it occurs. He is not far away. He whose eye is on the sparrow is also upon His saints. His presence which fills immensity is always where His saints are. "Certainly I will be with thee," is the word of God to every child of His.

"The angel of the Lord encampeth round about them that fear him, and delivereth them" (Ps. 34:7). And nothing can touch those who fear God, only with the permission of the angel of the Lord. Nothing can break through the encampment without the permission of the captain of the Lord's hosts. Sorrows, afflictions, want, trouble, or even death, cannot enter this divine encampment without the consent of almighty God, and even then it is to be used by God in His plans for the good of His saints and for carrying out His plans and purposes:

> For I am persuaded, that neither death, nor life, nor angels, nor principalities, nor powers, nor things present, nor things to come,
>
> Nor height, nor depth, nor any other creature, shall be able to separate us from the love of God, which is in Christ Jesus our Lord (Rom 8:38, 39).

These evil things, unpleasant and afflictive, may come with divine permission, but God is on the spot, His hand is in all of them, and He sees to it that they are woven into His plans. He causes them to be overruled for the good of His people, and eternal good is brought out of them. These things, with hundreds of others, belong to the disciplinary processes of almighty God in administering His government for the children of men.

The providence of God reaches as far as the realm of prayer. It has to do with everything for which we pray.

Nothing is too small for the eye of God, nothing too insignificant for His notice and His care. God's providence has to do with even the stumbling of the feet of His saints:

> For he shall give his angels charge over thee, to keep thee in all thy ways.

> They shall bear thee up in their hands, lest thou dash thy foot against a stone (Ps. 91:11, 12).

Read again our Lord's words about the sparrow, for He says, ". . . five sparrows are [sold] for two farthings, and not one of them is forgotten before God" (Luke 12:6). Paul asks the pointed question, "Doth God take care for oxen?" His care reaches to the smallest things and has to do with the most insignificant matters which concern men. He who believes in the God of providence is prepared to see His hand in all things which come to him, and can pray over everything.

Not that the saint who trusts the God of providence, and who takes all things to God in prayer, can explain the mysteries of divine providence, but the praying ones recognize God in everything, see Him in all that comes to them, and are ready to say as John said to Peter at the Sea of Galilee, "It is the Lord."

Praying saints do not presume to interpret God's dealings with them nor undertake to explain God's providences, but they have learned to trust God in the dark as well as in the light, to have faith in God even when "cares like a wild deluge come, and storms of sorrow fall."

"Though he slay me, yet will I trust him." Praying saints rest themselves upon the words of Jesus to Peter, "What I do thou knowest not now, but thou shalt know hereafter." None but the praying ones can see God's hands in the providences of life. "Blessed are the pure in heart: for they shall see God," shall see God here in His providences, in His Word, in His church. These are they who do not rule God out of earth's affairs, and who believe God interferes with matters of earth for them.

While God's providence is over all men, yet His supervision and administration of His government are peculiarly in the interest of His people.

Prayer brings God's providence into action. Prayer puts God to work in overseeing and directing earth's affairs for the good of men. Prayer opens the way when it is shut up or straitened.

Providence deals more especially with temporalities. It is in this realm that the providence of God shines brightest and is most apparent. It has to do with food and raiment, with business difficulties, with strangely interposing and saving from danger, and with helping in emergencies at very opportune and critical times.

The feeding of the Israelites during the wilderness journey is a striking illustration of the providence of God in taking care of the temporal wants of His people. His dealings with those people show how He provided for them in that long pilgrimage.

> Day by day the manna fell,
> O to learn this lesson well!
> Still by constant mercy fed,
> Give me, Lord, my daily bread.
>
> Day by day the promise reads,
> Daily strength for daily needs;
> Cast forboding fears away,
> Take the manna of to-day.

Our Lord teaches this same lesson of a providence which clothes and feeds His people, in the Sermon on the Mount, when He says, "Take no thought . . . what ye shall eat, or what ye shall drink; nor yet for your body, what ye shall put on" (see Matt. 6:25). Then He directs attention to the fact that it is God's providence which feeds the fowls of the air, clothes the lilies of the field, and asks if God does all this for birds and flowers, will He not care for them?

All of this teaching leads up to the need of a childlike, implicit trust in an overruling providence, which looks after the temporal wants of the children of men. And let it be noted specially that all this teaching stands closely connected in the utterances of our Lord with what He says about prayer, thus closely connecting a divine oversight with prayer and its promises.

We have an impressive lesson on divine providence in the case of Elijah when he was sent to the brook Cherith, where God actually employed the ravens to feed His prophet. Here was an interposition so plain that God cannot be ruled out of life's temporalities. Before God will allow His servant to want bread, He moves the birds of the air to do His bidding and take care of His prophet.

Nor was this all. When the brook ran dry, God sent him to a poor widow, who had just enough meal and oil for the urgent needs of the good woman and her son. Yet she divided with him her last morsel of bread. What was the result? The providence of God interposed, and as long as the drought lasted, the cruse of oil never failed nor did the meal in the barrel give out.

The Old Testament sparkles with illustrations of the provisions of almighty God for His people, and shows clearly God's overruling providence. In fact the Old Testament is largely the account of a providence which dealt with a peculiar people, anticipating their every temporal

want, which ministered to them when in emergencies,
and which sanctified to them their troubles.

It is worthwhile to read that old hymn of Newton's
which has in it so much of the providence of God:

> Though troubles assail, and dangers affright,
> Though friends should all fail, and foes all unite,
> Yet one thing secures me, whatever betide,
> The promise assures us, the Lord will provide.
>
> The birds without barns, or storehouse are fed,
> From them let us learn, to trust for our bread;
> His saints what is fitting, shall ne'er be denied,
> So long as it's written, the Lord will provide.

In fact many of our old hymns are filled with senti-
ments in song about a divine providence, which are
worthwhile to be read and sung even in this day.

God is in the most afflictive and sorrowing events of
life. All such events are subjects of prayer, and this is so
for the reason that everything which comes into the life
of the praying one is in the providence of God and takes
place under His superintending hand. Some would rule
God out of the sad and hard things of life. They tell us
that God has nothing to do with certain events which
bring such grief to us. They say that God is not in the
death of children, that they die from natural causes, and
that it is but the working of natural laws.

Let us ask what are nature's laws but the laws of God,
the laws by which God rules the world? And what is
nature anyway? And who made nature? How great the
need to know that God is above nature, is in control of
nature, and is in nature? We need to know that nature
or natural laws are but the servants of almighty God who
made these laws, and that He is directly in them, and
they are but the divine servants to carry out God's gra-

cious designs, and are made to execute His gracious purposes. The God of providence, the God to whom the Christians pray, and the God who interposes in behalf of the children of men for their good, is above nature, in perfect and absolute control of all that belongs to nature. And no law of nature can crush the life out of even a child without God giving His consent, and without such a sad event occurring directly under His all-seeing eye, and without His being immediately present.

David believed this doctrine when he fasted and prayed for the life of his child, for why pray and fast for a baby to be spared if God has nothing to do with its death should it die?

Moreover, "does care for oxen," and have a direct oversight of the sparrows which fall to the ground, and yet have nothing to do with the going out of this world of an immortal child? Still further, the death of a child, no matter if it should come alone as some people claim by the operation of the laws of nature, let it be kept in mind that it is a great affliction to the parents of the child. Where do these innocent parents come in under any such doctrine? It becomes a great sorrow to mother and father. Are they not to recognize the hand of God in the death of the child? And is there no providence or divine oversight in the taking away of their child to them? David recognized the facts clearly that God had to do with keeping his child in life; that prayer might avail in saving his child from death, and that when the child died it was because God had ordered it. Prayer and providence in all this affair worked in harmonious co-operation, and David thoroughly understood it. No child ever dies without the direct permission of almighty God, and such an event takes place in His providence for wise and beneficent ends. God works it into His plans concerning the child himself and the parents and all concerned. Moreover, it is a subject of prayer whether the child lives or dies.

> In each event of life how clear,
>   Thy ruling hand I see;
> Each blessing to my soul most dear,
>   Because conferred by Thee.